# Chalet
## Cabled Sweaters
by Knit Picks

Photography by John Cranford
Graphic Design by Lee Meredith

Printed in the United States of America
Second Printing, 2022

ISBN 978-1-62767-278-8

Versa Press, Inc.

800-447-7829
www.versapress.com

# CONTENTS

# AXIOM

by Claire Slade

### FINISHED MEASUREMENTS

34.75 (38.25, 41.75, 45.25, 49)(53, 56.25, 59.75, 63.25)" finished chest circumference, meant to be worn with 3" positive ease

*Sample on woman is 38.25" size and model is 31" chest; sample on man is 45.25" size and model is 38" chest*

### YARN

Wool of the Andes™ (worsted weight, 100% Peruvian Highland Wool; 110 yards/50g): Depths 28283 *or* Fjord Heather 25647, 10 (11, 13, 14, 16)(17, 18, 20, 21) skeins

### NEEDLES

US 8 (5mm) straight or circular needles, or size to obtain gauge
US 8 (5mm) 16" circular needles, or size to obtain gauge

### NOTIONS

Yarn Needle
Stitch Markers
Cable Needle
Scrap Yarn or Stitch Holders
Blocking Pins and/or Wires

### GAUGE

18 sts and 24 rows = 4" in Stockinette Stitch, blocked
25 sts and 24 rows = 4" in Cable Pattern, blocked

For pattern support, contact verilyknits@gmail.com

# Axiom

*Notes:*

Axiom is a classic shaped, completely unisex cable-front sweater suitable for anyone who loves coziness. With all sections worked from the bottom up, it is easy to knit this sweater to the perfect length.

Axiom is knit flat. Once all of the pieces have been knit, they are seamed together and stitches are picked up for the ribbed neckline. There are different cable instructions for the smaller sizes and the larger sizes.

Charts are worked flat; read RS rows (odd numbers) from right to left, and WS rows (even numbers) from left to right.

## 2/2 RC (Cable 2 Over 2 Right)
Sl2 to CN, hold in back; K2, K2 from CN.

## 2/2 LC (Cable 2 Over 2 Left)
Sl2 to CN, hold in front; K2, K2 from CN.

## Rib Pattern (flat over a multiple of 4 sts plus 2)
**Row 1 (RS):** K2, (P2, K2) to end.
**Row 2 (WS):** P2 (K2, P2) to end.
Rep Rows 1–2 for pattern.

## Cable Pattern A (flat over 50 sts)
**Row 1 (RS):** P2, 2/2 LC, P2, 2/2 RC, P2, K4, 2/2 RC, K2, P2, K2, 2/2 LC, K4, P2, 2/2 LC, P2, 2/2 RC, P2.
**Row 2 and all WS Rows:** (K2, P4) two times, (K2, P10) two times, (K2, P4) two times, K2.
**Row 3:** P2, 2/2 LC, P2, 2/2 RC, P2, K2, 2/2 RC, K4, P2, K4, 2/2 LC, K2, P2, 2/2 LC, P2, 2/2 RC, P2.
**Row 5:** P2, 2/2 LC, P2, 2/2 RC, P2, 2/2 RC, K2, 2/2 RC, P2, 2/2 LC, K2, 2/2 LC, P2, 2/2 LC, P2, 2/2 RC, P2.
Rep Rows 1–6 for pattern.

## Cable Pattern B (flat over 62 sts)
**Row 1 (RS):** P2, 2/2 RC, P2, 2/2 LC, P2, 2/2 RC, P2, K4, 2/2 RC, K2, P2, K2, 2/2 LC, K4, P2, 2/2 LC, P2, 2/2 RC, P2, 2/2 LC, P2.
**Row 2 and all WS Rows:** (K2, P4) three times, (K2, P10) two times, (K2, P4) three times, K2.
**Row 3:** P2, 2/2 RC, P2, 2/2 LC, P2, 2/2 RC, P2, K2, 2/2 RC, K4, P2, K4, 2/2 LC, K2, P2, 2/2 LC, P2, 2/2 RC, P2, 2/2 LC, P2.
**Row 5:** P2, 2/2 RC, P2, 2/2 LC, (P2, 2/2 RC) two times, K2, 2/2 RC, P2, 2/2 LC, K2, (2/2 LC, P2) two times, 2/2 RC, P2, 2/2 LC, P2.
Rep Rows 1–6 for pattern.

# DIRECTIONS

## Front

### Lower Edge
Loosely CO 94 (102, 110, 118, 130)(138, 146, 154, 162) sts.
Work Rows 1–2 of Rib Pattern until work measures 2", ending on a WS row.

## Body Setup
### Sizes 34.75 (38.25, 41.75, 45.25, -)(-, -, -, -)" Only
**Setup Row 1 (RS):** K22 (26, 30, 34, -)(-, -, -, -), PM, P2, 2/2 LC, P2, 2/2 RC, P2, K6, 2/2 RC, P2, 2/2 LC, K6, P2, 2/2 LC, P2, 2/2 RC, P2, PM, K to end.
**Setup Row 2 (WS):** P to M, SM, (K2, P4) two times, (K2, P10) two times, (K2, P4) two times, K2, SM, P to end.

### Sizes - (-, -, -, 49)(53, 56.25, 59.75, 63.25)" Only
**Setup Row 1 (RS):** K- (-, -, -, 34)(38, 42, 46, 50), PM, P2, 2/2 RC, P2, 2/2 LC, P2, 2/2 RC, P2, K6, 2/2 RC, P2, 2/2 LC, K6, P2, 2/2 LC, P2, 2/2 RC, P2, 2/2 LC, P2, PM, K to end.
**Setup Row 2 (WS):** P to M, SM, (K2, P4) three times, (K2, P10) two times, (K2, P4) three times, K2, SM, P to end.

## Body
Sizes 34.75 (38.25, 41.75, 45.25, -)(-, -, -, -)" use Cable Pattern A.
Sizes - (-, -, -, 49)(53, 56.25, 59.75, 63.25)" use Cable Pattern B.

**All RS Rows:** K to M, SM, work Cable Pattern to M, SM, K to end.
**All WS Rows:** P to M, SM, work Cable Pattern to M, SM, P to end.
Rep these two Rows until work measures 16 (16, 17, 17, 17.5)(17.5, 18, 18, 18.5)" from CO edge or desired length to underarm.

**Next Two Rows:** BO 4 (4, 4, 4, 6)(8, 8, 10, 10) sts, work to end. 86 (94, 102, 110, 118)(122, 130, 134, 142) sts.
WE as established until work measures 5.5 (6, 6.5, 7.5, 8)(8.5, 9, 9, 9.5)" from underarm BO, ending on a WS row.
**Next Row (RS):** Work across first 31 (35, 39, 43, 42)(44, 48, 50, 54) sts and place on st holder or scrap yarn for left front, BO next 24 (24, 24, 24, 34)(34, 34, 34, 34) sts, work to end. 31 (35, 39, 43, 42)(44, 48, 50, 54) right front sts.

## Right Front
If a full cable cannot be completed, work St st.

### First Decrease Section
**Row 1 (WS):** Work to end.
**Row 2 (RS):** BO 2 sts, work to end. 2 sts dec.
Rep Rows 1–2 another 0 (1, 2, 2, 1)(1, 2, 2, 2) times.
29 (31, 33, 37, 38)(40, 42, 44, 48) sts.

### Second Decrease Section
**Row 1 (WS):** Work to end.
**Row 2 (RS):** SSK, work to end. 1 st dec.
Rep Rows 1–2 another 5 (5, 5, 5, 4)(4, 4, 4, 4) times.
23 (25, 27, 31, 33)(35, 37, 39, 43) sts.
Work St st for 4 (2, 0, 0, 4)(4, 2, 2, 2) rows.

### Shoulder
**Row 1 (WS):** BO 11 (12, 13, 15, 16)(17, 18, 19, 21) sts, P to end.
**Row 2 (RS):** K across.
BO remaining 12 (13, 14, 16, 17)(18, 19, 20, 22) sts.

## Left Front
If a full cable cannot be completed, work St st.
With WS facing, return held sts to needle and rejoin yarn.

### First Decrease Section
**Row 1 (WS):** BO 2 sts, work to end. 2 sts dec.
**Row 2 (RS):** Work to end.
Rep Rows 1–2 another 0 (1, 2, 2, 1)(1, 2, 2, 2) times.
29 (31, 33, 37, 38)(40, 42, 44, 48) sts.

### Second Decrease Section
**Row 1 (WS):** Work to end.
**Row 2 (RS):** Work to last 2 sts, K2tog. 1 st dec.
Rep Rows 1–2 another 5 (5, 5, 5, 4)(4, 4, 4, 4) times.
23 (25, 27, 31, 33)(35, 37, 39, 43) sts.
Work St st for 5 (3, 1, 1, 5)(5, 3, 3, 3) rows.

### Shoulder
**Row 1 (RS):** BO 11 (12, 13, 15, 16)(17, 18, 19, 21) sts, K to end.
**Row 2 (RS):** P across.
BO remaining 12 (13, 14, 16, 17)(18, 19, 20, 22) sts.

## Back
### Lower Edge
CO 78 (86, 94, 102, 110)(122, 126, 134, 142) sts.
Work Rows 1–2 of Rib Pattern until work measures 2″,
ending on a WS row.

### Body
**Sizes 34.75 (38.25, 41.75, 45.25, 49)(-, 56.25, 59.75, 63.25)″ Only**
**Setup Row (RS):** K1, KFB, K to last 2 sts, KFB, K1. 80 (88, 96,
104, 112)(-, 128, 136, 144) sts.

### Resume All Sizes
Work St st until work measures 16 (16, 17, 17, 17.5)(17.5, 18, 18,
18.5)″ from CO edge.
**Next Two Rows:** BO 4 (4, 4, 4, 6)(8, 8, 10, 10) sts, work to
end. 72 (80, 88, 96, 100)(106, 112, 116, 124) sts.
WE as established until work measures 7.75 (8.25, 8.5, 9.5,
10)(10.5, 11, 11, 11.5)″ from underarm BO, ending on a WS row.
**Next Row (RS):** K25 (27, 30, 34, 36)(38, 40, 42, 46) and
place on st holder or scrap yarn for right back, BO next 22
(26, 28, 28, 28)(30, 32, 32, 32) sts, K to end. 25 (27, 30, 34,
36)(38, 40, 42, 46) sts.

### Left Back
**Row 1 (WS):** P across.
**Row 2 (RS):** SSK, K to end. 1 st dec.
Rep Rows 1–2 another 1 (1, 2, 2, 2)(2, 2, 2, 2) times.
23 (25, 27, 31, 33)(35, 37, 39, 43) sts.

### Shoulder
**Row 1 (WS):** BO 11 (12, 13, 15, 16)(17, 18, 19, 21) sts, P to end.
**Row 2 (RS):** K across.
BO remaining 12 (13, 14, 16, 17)(18, 19, 20, 22) sts.

### Right Back
With WS facing, return held sts to needle and rejoin yarn.
**Row 1 (WS):** P across.
**Row 2 (RS):** K to last 2 sts, K2tog. 1 st dec.
Rep Rows 1–2 another 1 (1, 2, 2, 2)(2, 2, 2, 2) times.
23 (25, 27, 31, 33)(35, 37, 39, 43) sts.

### Shoulder
**Row 1 (WS):** P across.
**Row 2 (RS):** BO 11 (12, 13, 15, 16)(17, 18, 19, 21) sts, K to end.
**Row 3:** P across.
BO remaining 12 (13, 14, 16, 17)(18, 19, 20, 22) sts.

## Sleeves
### Lower Edge
Loosely CO 38 (42, 42, 46, 50)(50, 50, 50, 54) sts.
Work Rows 1–2 of Rib Pattern until work measures 2″,
ending on a WS row.

### Main Section
Starting with a RS row, work St st for four rows.

**Sizes - (-, -, 45.25, 49)(53, 56.25, 59.75, 63.25)″ Only**
**Row 1 (RS):** K1, M1, K to last st, M1, K1. 2 sts inc.
**Row 2 (WS):** P across.
Rep Rows 1–2 another - (-, -, 4, 4)(7, 11, 11, 11) times.
- (-, -, 56, 60)(66, 74, 74, 78) sts.

### Resume All Sizes
**Row 1 (RS):** K1, M1, K to last st, M1, K1. 2 sts inc.
Work St st for three rows.
Rep these four rows 18 (18, 20, 19, 18)(18, 16, 16, 16) more
times. 76 (80, 84, 96, 98)(104, 108, 108, 112) sts.
WE in St st until sleeve measures 19 (19, 19.5, 19.5, 19.5)(20,
20, 20.5, 20.5)″, or until desired length, ending on a RS row.
BO all sts.

Wash and block all pieces to diagram.
Sew both side seams and both shoulder seams. Sew both
sleeves into armholes and sew up sleeve seams.

## Neckline
Starting at top LH shoulder with RS facing, using shorter
circular needle, rejoin yarn and PU and K: 15 sts down left
front, 24 (24, 24, 24, 34)(34, 34, 34, 34) sts across front BO,
15 sts up right front, 4 (4, 5, 5, 6)(5, 6, 6, 6) sts down right
back, 22 (26, 28, 28, 28)(30, 32, 32, 32) sts across back BO,
and 4 (4, 5, 5, 6)(5, 6, 6, 6) sts up left back. Join to work in
the rnd. 84 (88, 92, 92, 104)(104, 108, 108, 108) sts.
**Rnd 1:** (K2, P2) to end.
Rep Rnd 1 until ribbing measures 1″.
BO all sts loosely in pattern.

## Finishing
Weave in ends. Wash and block again lightly if desired.

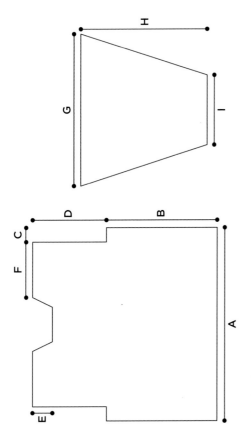

A *body width* 17.75 (19.5, 21.25, 23, 25)(27, 28.5, 30.5, 32)"
B *length to underarm* 16 (16, 17, 17, 17.5)(17.5, 18, 18, 18.5)"
C *underarm indent width* 1 (1, 1, 1.25)(1.75, 1.75, 2.25, 2.25)"
D *armhole depth* 8.5 (9, 9.5, 10.5, 11)(11.5, 12, 12, 12.5)"
E *front neck depth* 3.25"
F *shoulder width* 5 (5.5, 6, 7, 7.25)(7.75, 8.25, 8.75, 9.5)"
G *upper sleeve width* 17 (17.75, 18.75, 21.25, 21.75)(23, 24, 24, 25)"
H *sleeve length* 19 (19, 19.5, 19.5, 19.5)(20, 20, 20.5, 20.5)"
I *cuff width* 8.5 (9.25, 9.25, 10.25, 11)(11, 11, 11, 12)"

## LEGEND

K
RS: Knit stitch
WS: Purl stitch

P
RS: Purl stitch
WS: Knit stitch

**Cable 2 Over 2 Right (2/2 RC)**
Sl2 to CN, hold in back; K2, K2 from CN

**Cable 2 Over 2 Left (2/2 LC)**
Sl2 to CN, hold in front; K2, K2 from CN

## Cable Pattern A

## Cable Pattern B

# CARTWHEELS

by Rita Taylor

## FINISHED MEASUREMENTS

33.25 (37.25, 41.25, 45.25)(49.25, 53.25, 57.25, 61.25)" finished chest circumference, meant to be worn with 6" positive ease
*Sample is 37.25" size; model is 31" chest*

## YARN

Wool of the Andes™ (worsted weight, 100% Peruvian Highland Wool); 110 yards/50g): Cilantro Heather 25635, 13 (14, 16, 17)(19, 19, 20, 21) skeins

## NEEDLES

US 8 (5mm) straight or circular needles (24" or longer), or size to obtain gauge

US 6 (4mm) 24" circular needles plus optional straight needles (if preferred for knitting flat), or two sizes smaller than size used to obtain gauge

## NOTIONS

Yarn Needle
Stitch Markers
Cable Needle
Stitch Holders or Scrap Yarn

## GAUGE

20 sts and 24 rows = 4" in Double Moss Stitch, blocked
74-st wide center panel = 12.25", blocked
26-st wide cable at center of sleeve = 4.75", blocked

For pattern support, contact k2togp1@btinternet.com

# Cartwheels

*Notes:*

This pattern was inspired by the design of a wheel on a farm gate. The shape, with the saddle shoulders and straight armholes, is one that would be found in most rural areas of the northern hemisphere. It is reminiscent of the smocks worn by agricultural workers in parts of Europe.

Cartwheels is worked flat from the bottom up with Double Moss Stitch texture and cables throughout. Saddle shoulders give it a special touch, with the cable design running all the way up to the neckband.

Charts are worked flat; read RS rows (odd numbers) from right to left, and WS rows (even numbers) from left to right.

### Tw2R (Twist 2 Right)
K2tog, leaving sts on LH needle, K into first st again, drop both sts off LH needle.

### M1P (Make 1 Purl stitch)
Inserting LH needle from back to front, PU horizontal strand between st just worked and next st, and P.

### Cable Ribbing (flat over a multiple of 5 sts plus 3)
Row 1 (RS): K2, (P1, Tw2R , P1, K1) to last st, K1.
Row 2 (WS): K1, P1 (K1, P2, K1, P1) to last st, K1.
Rep Rows 1–2 for pattern.

### Double Moss Stitch (flat over a multiple of 2 sts)
Row 1 (RS): (K1 P1) to end.
Row 2 (WS): (P1, K1) to end.
Row 3: Rep Row 2.
Row 4: Rep Row 1.
Rep Rows 1–4 for pattern.

## DIRECTIONS

### Back
Using smaller needles, loosely CO 98 (108, 118, 128)(138, 148, 158, 168) sts.
Work Cable Ribbing for 2.5 (2.75, 2.75, 2.75)(3, 3, 3, 3)".

Change to larger needles.
Setup Row: (K1, P1) 6 (8, 11, 13)(16, 18, 21, 23) times, K0 (1, 0, 1)(0, 1, 0, 1), P1, K2, (P4, K4) two times, P4, K2, P4, K4, (P2, K4) two times, P4, K2, (P4, K4) two times, P4, K2, P1, K0 (1, 0, 1)(0, 1, 0, 1), (P1, K1) 6 (8, 11, 13)(16, 18, 21, 23) times.
Next Row: (P1, K1) 6 (8, 11, 13)(16, 18, 21, 23) times, P0 (1, 0, 1)(0, 1, 0, 1), K1, P2, (K4, P4) two times, K4, P2, K4, P4 (K2, P4) two times, K4, P2, (K4, P4) two times, K4, P2, K1, P0 (1, 0, 1)(0, 1, 0, 1), (K1, P1) 6 (8, 11, 13)(16, 18, 21, 23) times.

Begin working from charts as follows.
Work Double Moss Stitch over 12 (17, 22, 27)(32, 37, 42, 47) sts; work Row 1 of Chart C, Chart B, Chart C, Chart A, Chart C, Chart B, Chart C; work Double Moss Stitch over 12 (17, 22, 27)(32, 37, 42, 47) sts.
Cont as established until piece measures 13.5 (13.75, 14, 14.5)(14.75, 14.75, 15.5, 15.5)", or to desired length.

### Armhole Shaping
BO 8 (10, 12, 14)(15, 17, 19, 20) sts at beginning of next two rows. 82 (88, 94, 100)(108, 114, 120, 128) sts.
Cont in pattern as established until armhole measures 5.5 (6, 6, 6.5)(6.5, 6.75, 7, 7)" from BO sts.

### Neck Shaping
Work 26 (28, 29, 32)(35, 38, 40, 44) sts as established for shoulder, place 30 (32, 36, 36)(38, 38, 40, 40) sts on st holder or scrap yarn, work remaining 26 (28, 29, 32)(35, 38, 40, 44) sts of second shoulder as established.
Work these second shoulder sts as established for 1".
BO all second shoulder sts.

Return to first set of shoulder sts and work as established to match second shoulder.
BO shoulder sts.

### Front
Work Front the same as Back.

### Sleeves (make two the same)
Using smaller needles, CO 48 (48, 58, 58)(58, 58, 68, 68) sts.
Work Cable Ribbing for 2.5 (2.75, 2.75, 2.75)(2.5, 2.5, 3, 3)".

Change to larger needles.
Work Double Moss Stitch for 11 (11, 16, 16)(16, 16, 21, 21) sts; work across Chart C, Chart B, Chart C; work Double Moss Stitch for 11 (11, 16, 16)(16, 16, 21, 21) sts.
WE as established for three rows.

Work Inc Row as follows.
Inc Row (RS): K1, M1 or M1P to maintain established Double Moss Stitch pattern, work to last st as established, M1 or M1P in pattern, K1. 2 sts inc.
Work Inc Row every 4 (4, 4, 4)(3, 3, 3, 3) rows 14 (18, 17, 20)(23, 24, 21, 23) more times. 78 (86, 94, 100)(106, 108, 112, 116) sts.

Work as established until sleeve measures 17.5 (17.5, 18, 18.5)(18.5, 18, 19, 19)", or to desired length.
Saddle Shaping: BO 30 (34, 38, 41)(44, 44, 46, 48) sts at beginning of next two rows, keeping center 18 (18, 18, 18)(18, 20, 20, 20) sts in pattern as established.
Work remaining sts in pattern until saddle will fit along the 26 (28, 29, 32)(35, 38, 40, 44) sts of one shoulder: 4.5 (5, 5.25, 5.75)(6.5, 7, 7.5, 8.25)". Do not BO sts; place on st holder.

Sew saddles to shoulders, easing to fit.

### Neckband
Using smaller circular needles and starting at back of left shoulder, K18 (18, 18, 18)(18, 20, 20, 20) held sts from left saddle, PU and K 6 sts down side of left front neck, K30 (32, 36, 36)(38, 38, 40, 40) held sts from front neck, PU and K 6 sts along side of right front neck, K18 (18, 18, 18)(18, 20, 20, 20) held sts from right saddle, PU and K 6 sts along side of right back neck, K30 (32, 36, 36)(38, 38, 40, 40) held sts from back neck, PU and K 6 sts along side of left back neck.

120 (124, 132, 132)(136, 140, 144, 144) sts.
Work 1x1 Rib in the rnd for 1.25".
BO loosely.

## Finishing
Sew sleeves into armholes, easing to fit.
Sew side and sleeve seams.
Weave in all ends, wash, and block.

## LEGEND

| | |
|---|---|
| ☐ | **K** <br> RS: Knit stitch <br> WS: Purl stitch |
| ⊡ | **P** <br> RS: Purl stitch <br> WS: Knit stitch |
| | **Twist 2 Right (Tw2R)** <br> K2tog, leaving sts on LH needle, K into first st again, drop both sts off LH needle |
| | **Cable 2 Over 1 Right, Purl back (2/1 RPC)** <br> Sl1 to CN, hold in back; K2, P1 from CN |
| | **Cable 2 Over 1 Left, Purl back (2/1 LPC)** <br> Sl2 to CN, hold in front; P1, K2 from CN |
| | **Cable 2 Over 2 Right (2/2 RC)** <br> Sl2 to CN, hold in back; K2, K2 from CN |
| | **Cable 2 Over 2 Left (2/2 LC)** <br> Sl2 to CN, hold in front; K2, K2 from CN |
| | **Cable 2 Over 2 Right, Purl back (2/2 RPC)** <br> Sl2 to CN, hold in back; K2, P2 from CN |
| | **Cable 2 Over 2 Left, Purl back (2/2 LPC)** <br> Sl2 to CN, hold in front; P2, K2 from CN |

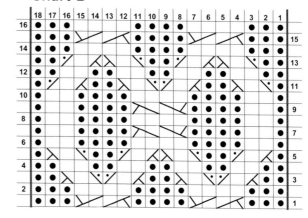

A  *chest circumference* 33.25 (37.25, 41.25, 45.25)(49.25, 53.25, 57.25, 61.25)"
B  *side seam* 13.5 (13.75, 14, 14.5)(14.75, 14.75, 15.5, 15.5)"
C  *armhole depth* 6.5 (7, 7, 7.5)(7.5, 7.75, 8, 8)"
D  *saddle shoulder height* 1.75 (1.75, 1.75, 1.75)(1.75, 2, 2, 2)"
E  *finished back length* 21.75 (22.5, 22.75, 23.75)(24, 24.5, 25.5, 25.5)"
F  *back neck width* 5 (5.5, 6.25, 6.25)(6.5, 6.5, 6.75, 6.75)"
G  *shoulder width/saddle length* 4.5 (5, 5.25, 5.75)(6.5, 7, 7.5, 8.25)"
H  *sleeve length* 17.5 (17.5, 18, 18.5)(18.5, 18, 19, 19)"
I  *saddle width* 3.25 (3.25, 3.25, 3.25)(3.25, 3.75, 3.75, 3.75)"
J  *cuff circumference (above ribbing)* 9.25 (9.25, 11.25, 11.25, 11.25)(11.25, 13.25, 13.25)"

## Chart B

| | 18 | 17 | 16 | 15 | 14 | 13 | 12 | 11 | 10 | 9 | 8 | 7 | 6 | 5 | 4 | 3 | 2 | 1 | |
|---|---|---|---|---|---|---|---|---|---|---|---|---|---|---|---|---|---|---|---|
| 16 | • | • | • | | | | | • | • | • | • | | | | | • | • | • | |
| | • | • | • | | | | • | • | • | • | • | | | | • | • | • | • | 15 |
| 14 | • | • | • | | | • | | | • | • | • | | | • | | | • | • | |
| | • | • | • | | | • | | | • | • | • | | | • | | | • | • | 13 |
| 12 | • | • | • | | | • | • | | • | • | • | | | • | • | | • | • | |
| | • | • | • | | | • | • | | • | • | • | | | • | • | | • | • | 11 |
| 10 | • | | | • | • | • | • | | | • | • | | | • | • | | | • | |
| | • | | | • | • | • | • | | | • | • | | | • | • | | | • | 9 |
| 8 | • | | | • | • | • | • | | | • | • | | | • | • | | | • | |
| | • | | | • | • | • | • | | | • | • | | | • | • | | | • | 7 |
| 6 | • | | | • | • | • | • | | | • | • | | | • | • | | | • | |
| | • | | | • | • | • | • | | | • | • | | | • | • | | | • | 5 |
| 4 | • | | | • | • | • | • | | | • | • | • | • | | | • | • | • | |
| | • | | | • | • | • | • | | | • | • | • | • | | | • | • | • | 3 |
| 2 | • | • | • | • | • | | | • | • | • | • | • | • | | | • | • | • | |
| | • | • | • | • | • | | | • | • | • | • | • | • | | | • | • | • | 1 |

## Chart A

| | 22 | 21 | 20 | 19 | 18 | 17 | 16 | 15 | 14 | 13 | 12 | 11 | 10 | 9 | 8 | 7 | 6 | 5 | 4 | 3 | 2 | 1 | |
|---|---|---|---|---|---|---|---|---|---|---|---|---|---|---|---|---|---|---|---|---|---|---|---|
| 16 | • | • | • | • | | | | • | • | • | | | | | • | • | • | | | • | • | • | |
| | • | • | • | • | | | | • | • | • | | | | | • | • | • | | | • | • | • | 15 |
| 14 | • | • | • | • | | | | • | • | • | | | | | • | • | • | | | • | • | • | |
| | • | | • | | | | | • | | • | | | | | • | | • | | | • | | • | 13 |
| 12 | • | | | • | • | • | • | | | | | | | | | | • | • | • | • | | • | |
| | • | | | • | • | • | • | | | | | | | | | | • | • | • | • | | • | 11 |
| 10 | • | | | • | • | • | • | | | | | | | | | | • | • | • | • | | • | |
| | • | | | • | • | • | • | | | | | | | | | | • | • | • | • | | • | 9 |
| 8 | • | | | • | • | • | • | | | | | | | | | | • | • | • | • | | • | |
| | • | | | • | • | • | • | | | | | | | | | | • | • | • | • | | • | 7 |
| 6 | • | | | • | • | • | • | | | | | | | | | | • | • | • | • | | • | |
| | • | | | • | • | • | | | | | | | | | | | • | • | • | • | | • | 5 |
| 4 | • | • | • | • | | | | • | • | • | | | | | • | • | • | | | • | • | • | |
| | • | • | • | • | | | | • | • | • | | | | | • | • | • | | | • | • | • | 3 |
| 2 | • | • | • | • | | | | • | • | • | | | | | • | • | • | | | • | • | • | |
| | • | • | • | • | | | | • | • | • | | | | | • | • | • | | | • | • | • | 1 |

## Chart C

| | 4 | 3 | 2 | 1 | |
|---|---|---|---|---|---|
| 4 | • | | | • | |
| | • | | | • | 3 |
| 2 | • | | | • | |
| | • | | | • | 1 |

# CRISSCROSS

by Helen Metcalfe

## FINISHED MEASUREMENTS

32 (35.5, 40, 43.5, 48)(51.5, 56, 59.5, 64)"
finished chest circumference, meant to
be worn with 2–4" positive ease
*Sample is 35.5" size; model is 31" chest*

## YARN

Swish™ (worsted weight, 100% Fine
Superwash Merino Wool; 110 yards/50g):
Dove Heather 25631, 10 (11, 12, 13, 14)
(15, 17, 18, 19) skeins

## NEEDLES

US 7 (4.5mm) straight or circular needles
(24" or longer), plus DPNs or two circular
needles for two circulars technique, or
size to obtain gauge
US 8 (5mm) straight or circular needles
(24" or longer) or size to obtain gauge

## NOTIONS

Yarn Needle
Stitch Marker
Cable Needle
Two Stitch Holders or Scrap Yarn
Blocking Pins and/or Wires

## GAUGE

18 sts and 24 rows = 4" in Stockinette
Stitch using larger needles, blocked
22 sts and 25 rnds = 4" in 1x1 Rib in the
round using smaller needles, blocked
(note that this is approximate due to the
amount of stretch in the ribbing)
Width of Charts A & C (37 sts) = 5.75"
using larger needles
Width of Chart B (22 sts) = 3.5" using
larger needles
Width of Sleeve Chart (21 sts) = 3.25"
using larger needles

For pattern support, contact hmetcalfe@hotmail.co.uk

# Crisscross

*Notes:*

Crisscross was inspired by classic fisherman's ganseys and Aran knitting. Playing with a mix of intricate stitches and differing textures, combined with a simple shape, results in this classic jumper.

Crisscross is worked flat in pieces, all from the bottom edge up. Pieces are then seamed and the neckband is picked up and worked in the round. The cable pattern is featured on the front and back with a smaller panel on the sleeves.

Charts are worked flat; read RS rows (odd numbers) from right to left, and WS rows (even numbers) from left to right.

### 2/1 RPC (2 Over 1 Right Cable, Purl back)
Place 1 st on CN and hold at back of work, K2 from LH needle then P1 from CN.

### 2/1 LPC (2 Over 1 Left Cable, Purl back)
Place 2 sts on CN and hold at front of work, P1 from LH needle then K2 from CN.

### 2/2 RC (2 Over 2 Right Cable)
Place 2 sts on CN and hold at back of work, K2 from LH needle then K2 from CN.

### 2/2 LC (2 Over 2 Left Cable)
Place 2 sts on CN and hold at front of work, K2 from LH needle then K2 from CN.

### 2/2 RPC (2 Over 2 Right Cable, Purl back)
Place 2 sts on CN and hold at back of work, K2 from LH needle then P2 from CN.

### 2/2 LPC (2 Over 2 Left Cable, Purl back)
Place 2 sts on CN and hold at front of work, P2 from LH needle then K2 from CN.

### Chart A (flat over 37 sts)
**Row 1 (RS):** P3, 2/1 RPC, 2/1 LPC, P5, K4, P2, 2/1 LPC, 2/1 RPC, 2/1 LPC, P2, K4, P2.
**Row 2 (WS):** K2, P4, K2, P2, K2, P4, K3, P4, K5, P2, K2, P2, K3.
**Row 3:** P2, 2/1 RPC, P2, 2/1 LPC, P4, 2/2 RC, P3, 2/2 RC, P2, K2, P2, 2/2 RC, P2.
**Row 4:** K2, P4, K2, P2, K2, P4, K3, P4, (K4, P2) two times, K2.
**Row 5:** P1, 2/1 RPC, P4, 2/1 LPC, P3, K4, P2, 2/1 RPC, 2/1 LPC, 2/1 RPC, P2, K4, P2.
**Row 6:** K2, P4, K3, P4, K2, P2, K2, P4, K3, P2, K6, P2, K1.
**Row 7:** 2/1 RPC, P6, 2/1 LPC, P2, 2/2 LC, P2, K2, P2, 2/2 LC, P3, 2/2 LC, P2.
**Row 8:** K2, P4, K3, P4, K2, P2, K2, P4, K2, P2, K8, P2.
Rep Rows 1–8 for pattern.

### Chart B (flat over 22 sts)
**Row 1 (RS):** P6, 2/2 RC, K2, 2/2 LC, P6.
**Row 2 (WS):** K6, P10, K6.
**Row 3:** P4, 2/2 RPC, K2, 2/2 RC, 2/2 LPC, P4.
**Row 4:** K4, P2, K2, P6, K2, P2, K4.
**Row 5:** P2, 2/2 RPC, P1, 2/1 RPC, K2, 2/1 LPC, P1, 2/2 LPC, P2.
**Row 6:** K2, P2, K3, (P2, K1) two times, P2, K3, P2, K2.

**Row 7:** 2/2 RPC, P2, 2/1 RPC, P1, K2, P1, 2/1 LPC, P2, 2/2 LPC.
**Row 8:** P2, K4, (P2, K2) two times, P2, K4, P2.
**Row 9:** K2, P3, 2/1 RPC, P2, K2, P2, 2/1 LPC, P3, K2.
**Row 10:** (P2, K3) four times, P2.
**Row 11:** 2/2 LPC, 2/1 RPC, P3, K2, P3, 2/1 LPC, 2/2 RPC.
**Row 12:** K2, P4, K4, P2, K4, P4, K2.
**Row 13:** P2, 2/2 RC, P4, K2, P4, 2/2 LC, P2.
**Row 14:** Rep Row 12.
**Row 15:** 2/2 RPC, 2/2 LPC, P2, K2, P2, 2/2 RPC, 2/2 LPC.
**Row 16:** Rep Row 8.
**Row 17:** K2, P4, 2/2 LPC, K2, 2/2 RPC, P4, K2.
**Row 18:** P2, K6, P6, K6, P2.
**Row 19:** 2/2 LPC, P4, 2/2 LC, K2, P4, 2/2 RPC.
**Row 20:** K2, P2, K4, P6, K4, P2, K2.
**Row 21:** P2, 2/2 LPC, P2, K2, 2/2 RC, P2, 2/2 RPC, P2.
**Row 22:** Rep Row 4.
**Row 23:** P4, 2/2 LPC, 2/2 LC, K2, 2/2 RPC, P4.
**Row 24:** Rep Row 2.
Rep Rows 1–24 for pattern.

### Chart C (flat over 37 sts)
**Row 1 (RS):** P2, K4, P2, 2/1 LPC, 2/1 RPC, 2/1 LPC, P2, K4, P5, 2/1 RPC, 2/1 LPC, P3.
**Row 2 (WS):** K3, P2, K2, P2, K5, P4, K2, P2, K2, P4, K3, P4, K2.
**Row 3:** P2, 2/2 RC, P3, 2/2 RC, P2, K2, P2, 2/2 RC, P4, 2/1 RPC, P2, 2/1 LPC, P2.
**Row 4:** K2, (P2, K4) two times, P4, K2, P2, K2, P4, K3, P4, K2.
**Row 5:** P2, K4, P2, 2/1 RPC, 2/1 LPC, 2/1 RPC, P2, K4, P3, 2/1 RPC, P4, 2/1 LPC, P1.
**Row 6:** K1, P2, K6, P2, (k3, p4) two times, K2, P2, K2, P4, K2.
**Row 7:** P2, 2/2 LC, P2, K2, P2, 2/2 LC, P3, 2/2 LC, P2, 2/1 RPC, P6, 2/1 LPC.
**Row 8:** P2, K8, P2, K2, P4, K3, P4, K2, P2, K2, P4, K2.
Rep Rows 1–8 for pattern.

### Sleeve Chart (flat over 21 sts)
*Note:* This chart is part of Chart A, designated by red box from st 15 up to and including st 35.
**Row 1 (RS):** K4, P2, 2/1 LPC, 2/1 RPC, 2/1 LPC, P2, K4.
**Row 2 (WS):** P4, K2, P2, K2, P4, K3, P4.
**Row 3:** 2/2 RC, P3, 2/2 RC, P2, K2, P2, 2/2 RC.
**Row 4:** P4, K2, P2, K2, P4, K3, P4.
**Row 5:** K4, P2, 2/1 RPC, 2/1 LPC, 2/1 RPC, P2, K4.
**Row 6:** P4, K3, P4, K2, P2, K2, P4.
**Row 7:** 2/2 LC, P2, K2, P2, 2/2 LC, P3, 2/2 LC.
**Row 8:** Rep Row 6.
Rep Rows 1–8 for pattern.

## DIRECTIONS

### Back
**Hem**
**Using smaller needles, loosely CO 72 (81, 90, 99, 108)(117, 126, 135, 144) sts.
Work 1x1 Rib for 1.75" from CO edge, ending after a RS row.

## Body

**Setup Row (WS):** Work 1x1 Rib for 7 (12, 1, 7, 10)(2, 5, 11, 14) sts, *M1, work Rib for 2 (2, 3, 3, 3)(4, 4, 4, 4) sts; rep from * to last 7 (13, 2, 8, 11)(3, 5, 12, 14) sts, M1, work Rib to end. 102 (110, 120, 128, 138)(146, 156, 164, 174) sts.
Switch to larger needles.

**Row 1 (RS):** P3 (7, 12, 16, 21)(25, 30, 34, 39), work Row 1 of Chart A (from chart or written instructions), work Row 1 of Chart B, work Row 1 of Chart C, P to end.

**Row 2 (WS):** K3 (7, 12, 16, 21)(25, 30, 34, 39), work Row 2 of Chart C, work Row 2 of Chart B, work Row 2 of Chart A, K to end.**

Cont as established until back measures 23.25 (23.5, 24.25, 25.5, 26.5)(28, 28.5, 29, 29.25)", ending after a WS row.

### Neckline

Cont as established and BO 5 (5, 6, 6, 7)(8, 9, 9, 10) sts at beginning of next 8 (4, 8, 2, 2)(8, 8, 2, 2) rows. 62 (90, 72, 116, 124)(82, 84, 146, 154) sts.

Cont as established and BO 6 (6, 7, 7, 8)(9, 10, 10, 11) sts at beginning of next 2 (6, 2, 8, 8)(2, 2, 8, 8) rows. 50 (54, 58, 60, 60)(64, 64, 66, 66) sts.

Place remaining sts on a st holder or scrap yarn.

## Front

### Hem & Body

Work as for Back from ** to **.
Cont as established until front measures 20 (20.25, 21, 22.25, 23.25)(24.75, 25.25, 25.75, 26)", ending after a WS row.

### Neckline

**Next Row (RS):** Work 43 (46, 50, 54, 59)(62, 67, 71, 76) sts, turn; now work these sts only. Place remaining 59 (64, 70, 74, 79)(84, 89, 93, 98) sts on st holder or scrap yarn.

Cont as established and BO 4 sts at beginning of next 1 (1, 1, 2, 2)(2, 2, 2, 2) WS rows. 39 (42, 46, 46, 51)(54, 59, 63, 68) sts.
Cont as established and BO 3 sts at beginning of next WS row. 36 (39, 43, 43, 48)(51, 56, 60, 65) sts.
Cont as established and BO 2 sts at beginning of next 2 (3, 4, 2, 2)(3, 3, 4, 4) WS rows. 32 (33, 35, 39, 44)(45, 50, 52, 57) sts.

**Next Row (RS):** Work as established to last 3 sts, K2tog, K1. 1 st dec.
WE for one row.
Rep last two rows 5 (4, 3, 4, 4)(3, 3, 2, 2) more times. 26 (28, 31, 34, 39)(41, 46, 49, 54) sts.

Cont as established and BO 5 (5, 6, 6, 7)(8, 9, 9, 10) sts at beginning of next 4 (2, 4, 1, 1)(4, 4, 1, 1) RS rows, then BO 6 (6, 7, 7, 8)(9, 10, 10, 11) sts at beginning of next 1 (3, 1, 4, 4) (1, 1, 4, 4) RS rows. All sts have been bound off.

With RS facing, leave center 16 (18, 20, 20, 20)(22, 22, 22, 22) sts on holder and place 43 (46, 50, 54, 59)(62, 67, 71, 76) sts back onto larger needles.
Cont as established and BO 4 sts at beginning of next 1 (1, 1, 2, 2)(2, 2, 2, 2) RS rows. 39 (42, 46, 46, 51)(54, 59, 63, 68) sts.
Cont as established and BO 3 sts at beginning of next RS row. 36 (39, 43, 43, 48)(51, 56, 60, 65) sts.

Cont as established and BO 2 sts at beginning of next 2 (3, 4, 2, 2)(3, 3, 4, 4) RS rows. 32 (33, 35, 39, 44)(45, 50, 52, 57) sts.

WE for one row.

**Next Row (RS):** K1, SSK, work in pattern to end. 1 st dec.
Rep last two rows 5 (4, 3, 4, 4)(3, 3, 2, 2) more times. 26 (28, 31, 34, 39)(41, 46, 49, 54) sts.

WE for two rows.

Cont as established and BO 5 (5, 6, 6, 7)(8, 9, 9, 10) sts at beginning of next 4 (2, 4, 1, 1)(4, 4, 1, 1) WS rows, then BO 6 (6, 7, 7, 8)(9, 10, 10, 11) sts at beginning of next 1 (3, 1, 4, 4) (1, 1, 4, 4) WS rows. All sts have been bound off.

## Sleeves (make two the same)

Using smaller needles, loosely CO 38 (40, 44, 44, 48)(48, 50, 50, 50) sts.
Work 1x1 Rib for 1.5" from CO edge, ending after a RS row.

**Setup Row (WS):** Work 1x1 Rib for 1 (2, 4, 4, 3)(3, 4, 4, 4) sts, *M1, work Rib for 6 (6, 6, 6, 7)(7, 7, 7, 7) sts; rep from * to last 1 (2, 4, 4, 3)(3, 4, 4, 4) sts, M1, work Rib to end. 45 (47, 51, 51, 55)(55, 57, 57, 57) sts.
Switch to larger needles.

**Row 1 (RS):** P12 (13, 15, 15, 17)(17, 18, 18, 18), work Row 1 of Sleeve Chart (from chart red boxed sts or written instructions) to last 12 (13, 15, 15, 17)(17, 18, 18, 18) sts, P to end.

**Row 2 (WS):** K12 (13, 15, 15, 17)(17, 18, 18, 18), work Row 2 of Sleeve Chart to last 12 (13, 15, 15, 17)(17, 18, 18, 18) sts, K to end.

**Inc Row (RS):** P1, M1, work as established to last st, M1, P1. 2 sts inc.
WE as established for 11 (11, 11, 9, 7)(5, 3, 3, 3) rows.
Rep last 12 (12, 12, 10, 8)(6, 4, 4, 4) rows 6 (6, 6, 8, 10)(14, 17, 20, 20) more times. 59 (61, 65, 69, 77)(85, 93, 99, 99) sts.

Cont without shaping until work measures 18.25" or desired length from CO edge, ending after a WS row.
BO all sts.

## Neckband

Seam shoulders.
With RS facing and smaller needles, PU and K 19 sts down left front neckline; from front st holder, K1, *K2tog, K2 (1, 1, 1, 1)(1, 1, 1, 1); rep from * 2 (4, 4, 4, 4)(5, 5, 5, 5) more times, K2tog, K1 (0, 2, 2, 2)(1, 1, 1, 1), PU and K 19 sts up right front neckline; from back st holder, K4 (3, 2, 3, 3)(4, 4, 5, 5), *K2tog, K1; rep from * 13 (15, 17, 17, 17)(18, 18, 18, 18) more times, K4 (3, 2, 3, 3)(3, 3, 4, 4). PM to mark BOR. 86 (88, 92, 94, 94)(98, 98, 100, 100) sts.
Starting with a K st, work 1x1 Rib until Neckband measures 1".
BO loosely in pattern.

## Finishing

Line up center of top of sleeve cap with shoulder seam; sew tog using Mattress Stitch. Rep for other sleeve.
Sew sleeve and side seams.
Weave in ends, wash, and block to diagram.

## Chart A

| 37 | 36 | 35 | 34 | 33 | 32 | 31 | 30 | 29 | 28 | 27 | 26 | 25 | 24 | 23 | 22 | 21 | 20 | 19 | 18 | 17 | 16 | 15 | 14 | 13 | 12 | 11 | 10 | 9 | 8 | 7 | 6 | 5 | 4 | 3 | 2 | 1 |

Red Boxed sts are also used as Sleeve Chart

## Chart B

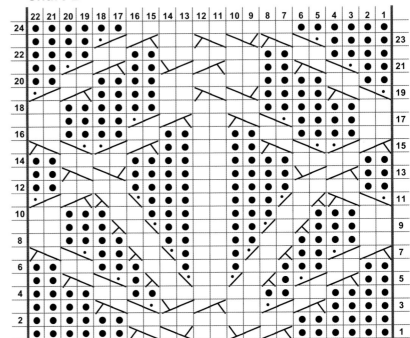

## LEGEND

K
RS: Knit stitch
WS: Purl stitch

P
RS: Purl stitch
WS: Knit stitch

Sleeve Chart Section

Cable 2 Over 1 Right, Purl back (2/1 RPC)
Sl1 to CN, hold in back; K2, P1 from CN

Cable 2 Over 1 Left, Purl back (2/1 LPC)
Sl2 to CN, hold in front; P1, K2 from CN

Cable 2 Over 2 Right (2/2 RC)
Sl2 to CN, hold in back; K2, K2 from CN

Cable 2 Over 2 Left (2/2 LC)
Sl2 to CN, hold in front; K2, K2 from CN

Cable 2 Over 2 Right, Purl back (2/2 RPC)
Sl2 to CN, hold in back; K2, P2 from CN

Cable 2 Over 2 Left, Purl back (2/2 LPC)
Sl2 to CN, hold in front; P2, K2 from CN

## Chart C

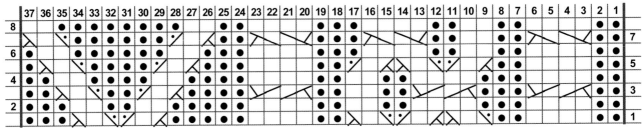

| 37 | 36 | 35 | 34 | 33 | 32 | 31 | 30 | 29 | 28 | 27 | 26 | 25 | 24 | 23 | 22 | 21 | 20 | 19 | 18 | 17 | 16 | 15 | 14 | 13 | 12 | 11 | 10 | 9 | 8 | 7 | 6 | 5 | 4 | 3 | 2 | 1 |

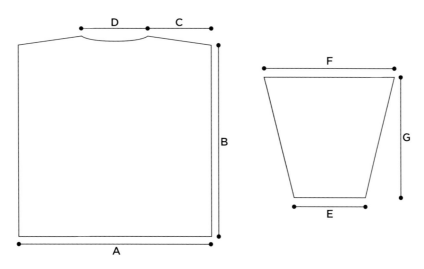

**A** *body width* 16.25 (18, 20.25, 22, 24.25)(26, 28.25, 30, 32.25)"
**B** *body length* 23.25 (23.5, 24.25, 25.5, 26.5)(28, 28.5, 29, 29.25)"
**C** *shoulder width* 4.25 (4.75, 5.5, 6.25, 7.5)(8, 9.25, 9.75, 11)"
**D** *back neck width* 7.75 (8.5, 9.25, 9.5, 9.25)(10, 9.75, 10.5, 10.25)"
**E** *cuff width* 8.5 (9, 10, 10, 10.75)(10.75, 11.25, 11.25, 11.25)"
**F** *top of sleeve width* 11.75 (12.25, 13, 14, 15.75)(17.5, 19.25, 20.5, 20.5)"
**G** *sleeve length* 18.25"

# DARA

by Ksenia Naidyon

## FINISHED MEASUREMENTS

To fit chest circumference up to
32 (34-44, 46-56, 58-68)"
*Sample is 34-44" size; model is 31" chest*

## YARN

Wool of the Andes™ Tweed (worsted
weight, 80% Peruvian Highland Wool,
20% Donegal Tweed; 110 yards/50g):
Picket Fence Heather 28309, 8 (14,
20, 28) skeins

## NEEDLES

US 6 (4mm) straight or circular needles
(24" or longer), or size to obtain gauge
US 4 (3.5mm) straight or circular needles
(24" or longer), or size to obtain Rib gauge
US 4 (3.5mm) 16" circular needles, or size
to obtain Rib gauge

## NOTIONS

Yarn Needle
Stitch Markers
Cable Needle
Blocking Pins and/or Wires

## GAUGE

25 sts and 30 rows = 4" in 2x2 Rib on
smaller needles, blocked (note that this
is approximate due to amount of stretch
in ribbing)
20 sts and 27 rows = 4" in Moss Stitch
on larger needles, blocked
25 sts and 27 rows = 4" in Cable Pattern
on larger needles, blocked (note that this
is approximate due to amount of stretch
in cables)

For pattern support, contact lifeiscozy@gmail.com

# Dara

*Notes:*

The inspiration for this piece was drawn from the ancient Celtic Dara knot. Meant to represent the root system of a sacred oak tree ("doire"), it is a symbol of wisdom and inner strength. Aran cables on the poncho intertwine, embellishing it with its very own Dara knots.

The body of the piece is knit flat as a rectangle with cables running along the edge. Once finished, it's folded in half and seamlessly joined with a cabled side panel. The neck opening is finished off with 2x2 Rib. Cabled panels are both charted and written.

Charts are worked flat; read RS rows (odd numbers) from right to left, and WS rows (even numbers) from left to right.

### RT (Right Twist)
Sl1 to CN, hold in back; K1, K1 from CN.

### 2/1 LPC (Cable 2 Over 1 Left, Purl back)
Sl2 to CN, hold in front; P1, K2 from CN.

### 2/1 RPC (Cable 2 Over 1 Right, Purl back)
Sl1 to CN, hold in back; K2, P1 from CN.

### 2/2 RC (Cable 2 Over 2 Right)
Sl2 to CN, hold in back; K2, K2 from CN.

### 3/1 LPC (Cable 3 Over 1 Left, Purl back)
Sl3 to CN, hold in front; P1, K3 from CN.

### 3/1 RPC (Cable 3 Over 1 Right, Purl back)
Sl1 to CN, hold in back; K3, P1 from CN.

### 3/2 LPC (Cable 3 Over 2 Left, Purl back)
Sl3 to CN, hold in front; P2, K3 from CN.

### 3/2 RPC (Cable 3 Over 2 Right, Purl back)
Sl2 to CN, hold in back; K3, P2 from CN.

### 3/3 LC (Cable 3 Over 3 Left)
Sl3 to CN, hold in front; K3, K3 from CN.

### 3/3 RC (Cable 3 Over 3 Right)
Sl3 to CN, hold in back; K3, K3 from CN.

### M1P (Make 1 Purl stitch)
Inserting LH needle from front to back, PU horizontal strand between st just worked and next st, and P TBL.

### 2x2 Rib with Selvage (flat over a multiple of 4 sts)
Row 1 (WS): Sl1, (P2, K2) to last 3 sts, P3.
Row 2 (RS): Sl1, (K2, P2) to last 3 sts, K3.
Rep Rows 1–2 for pattern.

### Moss Stitch (flat over an even number of sts)
Row 1 (RS): (K1, P1) to end.
Row 2 (WS): (P1, K1) to end.
Row 3: Rep Row 2.
Row 4: Rep Row 1.
Rep Rows 1–4 for pattern.

## Long Rectangle Chart (flat over 64 (64, 72, 72) sts)
Sts between * * are only worked for sizes 46–56" & 58–68".

Row 1 (RS): Sl1, RT, P3, 3/1 LPC, P3, 3/1 LPC, P4, 3/3 RC, P4, 3/1 RPC, P3, 3/1 RPC, P4, K4, P3, K2, P2, K2, P3, *K4, P4*, RT.

Row 2 (WS): P2, *K4, P4*, K3, P2, K2, P2, K3, P4, K5, (P3, K4) two times, P6, (K4, P3) three times.

Row 3: Sl1, RT, P4, K3, P4, (3/2 LPC, 3/2 RPC) two times, P4, K3, P5, 2/2 RC, P3, K2, P2, K2, P3, *2/2 RC, P4*, RT.

Row 4: P2, *K4, P4*, K3, P2, K2, P2, K3, P4, K5, P3, K6, P6, K4, P6, K6, P3, K4, P3.

Row 5: Sl1, RT, P4, 3/2 LPC, (P4, 3/3 LC) two times, P4, 3/2 RPC, P5, K4, P3, 2/1 LPC, 2/1 RPC, P3, *K4, P4*, RT.

Row 6: P2, (K4, P4) 2 (2, 3, 3) times, K7, P3, (K4, P6) two times, K4, P3, K6, P3.

Row 7: Sl1, RT, P6, (3/2 LPC, 3/2 RPC) three times, P7, (2/2 RC, P4) 2 (2, 3, 3) times, RT.

Row 8: P2, (K4, P4) 2 (2, 3, 3) times, K9, P6, (K4, P6) two times, K8, P3.

Row 9: Sl1, RT, P8, (3/3 RC, P4) three times, P4, 2/1 RPC, 2/1 LPC, P3, K4, P3, *2/1 RPC, 2/1 LPC, P2*, P1, RT.

Row 10: P2, K1, *(K2, P2) two times*, K3, P4, K3, P2, K2, P2, K8, (P6, K4) two times, P6, K8, P3.

Row 11: Sl1, RT, P6, (3/2 RPC, 3/2 LPC) three times, P6, K2, P2, K2, P3, 2/2 RC, P3, *(K2, P2) two times*, P1, RT.

Row 12: P2, K1, *(K2, P2) two times*, K3, P4, K3, P2, K2, P2, K6, P3, (K4, P6) two times, K4, P3, K6, P3.

Row 13: Sl1, RT, P6, K3, (P4, 3/3 LC) two times, P4, K3, P6, K2, P2, K2, P3, K4, P3, *(K2, P2) two times*, P1, RT.

Row 14: P2, K1, *(K2, P2) two times*, K3, P4, K3, P2, K2, P2, K6, P3, (K4, P6) two times, K4, P3, K6, P3.

Row 15: Sl1, RT, P6, (3/2 LPC, 3/2 RPC) three times, P6, K2, P2, K2, P3, 2/2 RC, P3, *(K2, P2) two times*, P1, RT.

Row 16: P2, K1, *(K2, P2) two times*, K3, P4, K3, P2, K2, P2, K8, (P6, K4) two times, P6, K8, P3.

Row 17: Sl1, RT, P8, (3/3 RC, P4) three times, P4, 2/1 LPC, 2/1 RPC, P3, K4, P3, *2/1 LPC, 2/1 RPC, P2*, P1, RT.

Row 18: P2, (K4, P4) 2 (2, 3, 3) times, K9, P6, (K4, P6) two times, K8, P3.

Row 19: Sl1, RT, P6, (3/2 RPC, 3/2 LPC) three times, P7, (2/2 RC, P4) 2 (2, 3, 3) times, RT.

Row 20: P2, (K4, P4) 2 (2, 3, 3) times, K7, P3, (K4, P6) two times, K4, P3, K6, P3.

Row 21: Sl1, RT, P4, 3/2 RPC, (P4, 3/3 LC) two times, P4, 3/2 LPC, P5, K4, P3, 2/1 RPC, 2/1 LPC, P3, *K4, P4*, RT.

Row 22: P2, *K4, P4*, K3, P2, K2, P2, K3, P4, K5, P3, K6, P6, K4, P6, K6, P3, K4, P3.

Row 23: Sl1, RT, P4, K3, P4, (3/2 RPC, 3/2 LPC) two times, P4, K3, P5, 2/2 RC, P3, K2, P2, K2, P3, *2/2 RC, P4*, RT.

Row 24: P2, *K4, P4*, K3, P2, K2, P2, K3, P4, K5, P3, K4, P3, K4, P6, (K4, P3) three times.

Row 25: Sl1, RT, (P3, 3/1 RPC) two times, P4, 3/3 RC, P4, 3/1 LPC, P3, 3/1 LPC, P4, K4, P3, K2, P2, K2, P3, *K4, P4*, RT.

Row 26: P2, *K4, P4*, K3, P2, K2, P2, K3, P4, (K4, P3) two times, K5, P6, K5, P3, K4, P3, K3, P3.

**Row 27:** Sl1, RT, P3, K3, P4, K3, P5, K6, P5, (K3, P4) two times, 2/2 RC, P3, K2, P2, K2, P3, *2/2 RC, P4*, RT.

**Row 28:** P2, *K4, P4*, K3, P2, K2, P2, K3, P4, (K4, P3) two times, K5, P6, K5, P3, K4, P3, K3, P3.

**Row 29:** Sl1, RT, P3, K3, P4, K3, P5, K6, P5, (K3, P4) two times, K4, P3, 2/1 LPC, 2/1 RPC, P3, *K4, P4*, RT.

**Row 30:** P2, (K4, P4) 2 (2, 3, 3) times, (K4, P3) two times, K5, P6, K5, P3, K4, P3, K3, P3.

**Row 31:** Sl1, RT, P3, K3, P4, K3, P5, 3/3 RC, P5, (K3, P4) two times, (2/2 RC, P4) 2 (2, 3, 3) times, RT.

**Row 32:** P2, (K4, P4) 2 (2, 3, 3) times, (K4, P3) two times, K5, P6, K5, P3, K4, P3, K3, P3.

**Row 33:** Sl1, RT, P3, (K3, P4) two times, 3/1 RPC, 3/1 LPC, (P4, K3) two times, P3, 2/1 RPC, 2/1 LPC, P3, K4, P3, *2/1 RPC, 2/1 LPC, P2*, P1, RT.

**Row 34:** P2, K1, *(K2, P2) two times*, K3, P4, K3, P2, K2, P2, K3, (P3, K4) two times, P3, K2, P3, (K4, P3) two times, K3, P3.

**Row 35:** Sl1, RT, P3, 3/2 LPC, 3/2 RPC, P3, 3/1 RPC, P2, 3/1 LPC, P3, 3/2 LPC, 3/2 RPC, P3, K2, P2, K2, P3, 2/2 RC, P3, *(K2, P2) two times*, P1, RT.

**Row 36:** P2, K1, *(K2, P2) two times*, K3, P4, K3, P2, K2, P2, K5, P6, K5, P3, K4, P3, K5, P6, K5, P3.

**Row 37:** Sl1, RT, P5, 3/3 RC, P5, K3, P4, K3, P5, 3/3 RC, P5, K2, P2, K2, P3, K4, P3, *(K2, P2) two times*, P1, RT.

**Row 38:** P2, K1, *(K2, P2) two times*, K3, P4, K3, P2, K2, P2, K5, P6, K5, P3, K4, P3, K5, P6, K5, P3.

**Row 39:** Sl1, RT, P3, 3/2 RPC, 3/2 LPC, P3, 3/1 LPC, P2, 3/1 RPC, P3, 3/2 RPC, 3/2 LPC, P3, K2, P2, K2, P3, 2/2 RC, P3, *(K2, P2) two times*, P1, RT.

**Row 40:** P2, K1, *(K2, P2) two times*, K3, P4, K3, P2, K2, P2, K3, P3, (K4, P3) two times, K2, P3, (K4, P3) two times, K3, P3.

**Row 41:** Sl1, RT, P3, (K3, P4) two times, 3/1 LPC, 3/1 RPC, (P4, K3) two times, P3, 2/1 LPC, 2/1 RPC, P3, K4, P3, *2/1 LPC, 2/1 RPC, P2*, P1, RT.

**Row 42:** P2, (K4, P4) 2 (2, 3, 3) times, (K4, P3) two times, K5, P6, K5, P3, K4, P3, K3, P3.

**Row 43:** Sl1, RT, P3, K3, P4, K3, P5, 3/3 RC, P5, (K3, P4) two times, (2/2 RC, P4) 2 (2, 3, 3) times, RT.

**Row 44:** P2, (K4, P4) 2 (2, 3, 3) times, (K4, P3) two times, K5, P6, K5, P3, K4, P3, K3, P3.

**Row 45:** Sl1, RT, P3, K3, P4, K3, P5, K6, P5, (K3, P4) two times, K4, P3, 2/1 RPC, 2/1 LPC, P3, *K4, P4*, RT.

**Row 46:** P2, *K4, P4*, K3, P2, K2, P2, K3, P4, (K4, P3) two times, K5, P6, K5, P3, K4, P3, K3, P3.

**Row 47:** Sl1, RT, P3, K3, P4, K3, P5, K6, P5, (K3, P4) two times, 2/2 RC, P3, K2, P2, K2, P3, *2/2 RC, P4*, RT.

**Row 48:** P2, *K4, P4*, K3, P2, K2, P2, K3, P4, (K4, P3) two times, K5, P6, K5, P3, K4, P3, K3, P3.

## Side Panel Chart (flat over 74 (74, 90, 90) sts)

Sts between * * are only worked for sizes 46–56" & 58–68".

**Row 1 (RS):** *P3, K4, P1*, (P2, K2) two times, P3, K4, P4, 3/1 LPC, P3, 3/1 LPC, P4, 3/3 RC, P4, 3/1 RPC, P3, 3/1 RPC, P4, K4, P3, (K2, P2) two times, *P1, K4, P3*.

**Row 2 (WS):** *K3, P4, K1*, (K2, P2) two times, K3, P4, K5, (P3, K4) two times, P6, (K4, P3) two times, K5, P4, K3, P2, K2, P2, K2, *K1, P4, K3*.

**Row 3:** *P3, 2/2 RC, P1*, (P2, K2) two times, P3, 2/2 RC, P5, K3, P4, (3/2 LPC, 3/2 RPC) two times, P4, K3, P5, 2/2 RC, P3, (K2, P2) two times, *P1, 2/2 RC, P3*.

**Row 4:** *K3, P4, K1*, (K2, P2) two times, K3, P4, K5, P3, K6, P6, K4, P6, K6, P3, K5, P4, K3, (P2, K2) two times, *K1, P4, K3*.

**Row 5:** *P3, K4, P1*, P2, 2/1 LPC, 2/1 RPC, P3, K4, P5, 3/2 LPC, (P4, 3/3 LC) two times, P4, 3/2 RPC, P5, K4, P3, 2/1 LPC, 2/1 RPC, P2, *P1, K4, P3*.

**Row 6:** *K3, P4, K1*, K3, P4, K4, P4, K7, P3, K4, (P6, K4) two times, P3, K7, P4, K4, P4, K3, *K1, P4, K3*.

**Row 7:** *P3, 2/2 RC, P1*, P3, 2/2 RC, P4, 2/2 RC, P7, (3/2 LPC, 3/2 RPC) three times, P7, 2/2 RC, P4, 2/2 RC, P3, *P1, 2/2 RC, P3*.

**Row 8:** *K3, P4, K1*, K3, P4, K4, P4, K9, (P6, K4) two times, P6, K9, P4, K4, P4, K3, *K1, P4, K3*.

**Row 9:** *P2, 2/1 RPC, 2/1 LPC*, P3, K4, P3, 2/1 RPC, 2/1 LPC, P8, (3/3 RC, P4) two times, 3/3 RC, P8, 2/1 RPC, 2/1 LPC, P3, K4, P3, *2/1 RPC, 2/1 LPC, P2*.

**Row 10:** *(K2, P2) two times*, K3, P4, K3, P2, K2, P2, K8, P6, (K4, P6) two times, K8, P2, K2, P2, K3, P4, K3, *(P2, K2) two times*.

**Row 11:** *(P2, K2) two times*, P3, 2/2 RC, P3, K2, P2, K2, P6, (3/2 RPC, 3/2 LPC) three times, P6, K2, P2, K2, P3, 2/2 RC, P3, *(K2, P2) two times*.

**Row 12:** *(K2, P2) two times*, K3, P4, K3, P2, K2, P2, K6, P3, (K4, P6) two times, K4, P3, K6, P2, K2, P2, K3, P4, K3, *(P2, K2) two times*.

**Row 13:** *(P2, K2) two times*, P3, K4, P3, K2, P2, K2, P6, K3, (P4, 3/3 LC) two times, P4, K3, P6, K2, P2, K2, P3, K4, P3, *(K2, P2) two times*.

**Row 14:** *(K2, P2) two times*, K3, P4, K3, P2, K2, P2, K6, P3, (K4, P6) two times, K4, P3, K6, P2, K2, P2, K3, P4, K3, *(P2, K2) two times*.

**Row 15:** *(P2, K2) two times*, P3, 2/2 RC, P3, K2, P2, K2, P6, (3/2 LPC, 3/2 RPC) three times, P6, K2, P2, K2, P3, 2/2 RC, P3, *(K2, P2) two times*.

**Row 16:** *(K2, P2) two times*, K3, P4, K3, P2, K2, P2, K8, (P6, K4) two times, P6, K8, P2, K2, P2, K3, P4, K3, *(P2, K2) two times*.

**Row 17:** *P2, 2/1 LPC, 2/1 RPC*, P3, K4, P3, 2/1 LPC, 2/1 RPC, P8, (3/3 RC, P4) two times, 3/3 RC, P8, 2/1 LPC, 2/1 RPC, P3, K4, P3, *2/1 LPC, 2/1 RPC, P2*.

**Row 18:** *K3, P4, K1*, K3, P4, K4, P4, K9, (P6, K4) two times, P6, K9, P4, K4, P4, K3, *K1, P4, K3*.

**Row 19:** *P3, 2/2 RC, P1*, P3, 2/2 RC, P4, 2/2 RC, P7, (3/2 RPC, 3/2 LPC) three times, P7, 2/2 RC, P4, 2/2 RC, P3, *P1, 2/2 RC, P3*.

**Row 20:** *K3, P4, K1*, K3, P4, K4, P4, K7, P3, (K4, P6) two times, K4, P3, K7, P4, K4, P4, K3, *K1, P4, K3*.

**Row 21:** *P3, K4, P1*, P2, 2/1 RPC, 2/1 LPC, P3, K4, P5, 3/2 RPC, (P4, 3/3 LC) two times, P4, 3/2 LPC, P5, K4, P3, 2/1 RPC, 2/1 LPC, P2, *P1, K4, P3*.

**Row 22:** *K3, P4, K1*, (K2, P2) two times, K3, P4, K5, P3, K6, P6, K4, P6, K6, P3, K5, P4, K3, (P2, K2) two times, *K1, P4, K3*.

**Row 23:** *P3, 2/2 RC, P1*, (P2, K2) two times, P3, 2/2 RC, P5, K3, P4, (3/2 RPC, 3/2 LPC) two times, P4, K3, P5, 2/2 RC, P3, (K2, P2) two times, *P1, 2/2 RC, P3*.

**Row 24:** *K3, P4, K1*, (K2, P2) two times, K3, P4, K5, (P3, K4) two times, P6, (K4, P3) two times, K5, P4, K3, (P2, K2) two times, *K1, P4, K3*.

**Row 25:** *P3, K4, P1*, (P2, K2) two times, P3, K4, P4, 3/1 RPC, P3, 3/1 RPC, P4, 3/3 RC, P4, 3/1 LPC, P3, 3/1 LPC, P4, K4, P3, (K2, P2) two times, *P1, K4, P3*.

**Row 26:** *K3, P4, K1*, (K2, P2) two times, K3, P4, (K4, P3) two times, K5, P6, K5, (P3, K4) two times, P4, K3, (P2, K2) two times, *K1, P4, K3*.

**Row 27:** *P3, 2/2 RC, P1*, (P2, K2) two times, P3, 2/2 RC, (P4, K3) two times, P5, K6, P5, (K3, P4) two times, 2/2 RC, P3, (K2, P2) two times, *P1, 2/2 RC, P3*.

**Row 28:** *K3, P4, K1*, (K2, P2) two times, K3, P4, (K4, P3) two times, K5, P6, K5, (P3, K4) two times, P4, K3, (P2, K2) two times, *K1, P4, K3*.

**Row 29:** *P3, K4, P1*, P2, 2/1 LPC, 2/1 RPC, P3, K4, (P4, K3) two times, P5, K6, P5, (K3, P4) two times, K4, P3, 2/1 LPC, 2/1 RPC, P2, *P1, K4, P3*.

**Row 30:** *K3, P4, K1*, K3, (P4, K4) two times, P3, K4, P3, K5, P6, K5, (P3, K4) two times, P4, K4, P4, K3, *K1, P4, K3*.

**Row 31:** *P3, 2/2 RC, P1*, P3, (2/2 RC, P4) two times, K3, P4, K3, P5, 3/3 RC, P5, K3, P4, K3, (P4, 2/2 RC) two times, P3, *P1, 2/2 RC, P3*.

**Row 32:** *K3, P4, K1*, K3, (P4, K4) two times, P3, K4, P3, K5, P6, K5, (P3, K4) two times, P4, K4, P4, K3, *K1, P4, K3*.

**Row 33:** *P2, 2/1 RPC, 2/1 LPC*, P3, K4, P3, 2/1 RPC, 2/1 LPC, P3, (K3, P4) two times, 3/1 RPC, 3/1 LPC, (P4, K3) two times, P3, 2/1 RPC, 2/1 LPC, P3, K4, P3, *2/1 RPC, 2/1 LPC, P2*.

**Row 34:** *(K2, P2) two times*, K3, P4, K3, P2, K2, P2, K3, (P3, K4) two times, P3, K2, (P3, K4) two times, P3, K3, P2, K2, P2, K3, P4, K3, *(P2, K2) two times*.

**Row 35:** *(P2, K2) two times*, P3, 2/2 RC, P3, K2, P2, K2, P3, 3/2 LPC, 3/2 RPC, P3, 3/1 RPC, P2, 3/1 LPC, P3, 3/2 LPC, 3/2 RPC, P3, K2, P2, K2, P3, 2/2 RC, P3, *(K2, P2) two times*.

**Row 36:** *(K2, P2) two times*, K3, P4, K3, P2, K2, P2, K5, P6, K5, P3, K4, P3, K5, P6, K5, P2, K2, P2, K3, P4, K3, *(P2, K2) two times*.

**Row 37:** *(P2, K2) two times*, P3, K4, P3, K2, P2, K2, P5, 3/3 RC, P5, K3, P4, K3, P5, 3/3 RC, P5, K2, P2, K2, P3, K4, P3, *(K2, P2) two times*.

**Row 38:** *(K2, P2) two times*, K3, P4, K3, P2, K2, P2, K5, P6, K5, P3, K4, P3, K5, P6, K5, P2, K2, P2, K3, P4, K3, *(P2, K2) two times*.

**Row 39:** *(P2, K2) two times*, P3, 2/2 RC, P3, K2, P2, K2, P3, 3/2 RPC, 3/2 LPC, P3, 3/1 LPC, P2, 3/1 RPC, P3, 3/2 RPC, 3/2 LPC, P3, K2, P2, K2, P3, 2/2 RC, P3, *(K2, P2) two times*.

**Row 40:** *(K2, P2) two times*, K3, P4, K3, P2, K2, P2, K3, (P3, K4) two times, P3, K2, (P3, K4) two times, P3, K3, P2, K2, P2, K3, P4, K3, *(P2, K2) two times*.

**Row 41:** *P2, 2/1 LPC, 2/1 RPC*, P3, K4, P3, 2/1 LPC, 2/1 RPC, P3, (K3, P4) two times, 3/1 LPC, 3/1 RPC, (P4, K3) two times, P3, 2/1 LPC, 2/1 RPC, P3, K4, P3, *2/1 LPC, 2/1 RPC, P2*.

**Row 42:** *K3, P4, K1*, K3, (P4, K4) two times, P3, K4, P3, K5, P6, K5, (P3, K4) two times, P4, K4, P4, K3, *K1, P4, K3*.

**Row 43:** *P3, 2/2 RC, P1*, P3, (2/2 RC, P4) two times, K3, P4, K3, P5, 3/3 RC, P5, K3, P4, K3, (P4, 2/2 RC) two times, P3, *P1, 2/2 RC, P3*.

**Row 44:** *K3, P4, K1*, K3, (P4, K4) two times, P3, K4, P3, K5, P6, K5, (P3, K4) two times, P4, K4, P4, K3, *K1, P4, K3*.

**Row 45:** *P3, K4, P1*, P2, 2/1 RPC, 2/1 LPC, P3, K4, (P4, K3) two times, P5, K6, P5, (K3, P4) two times, K4, P3, 2/1 RPC, 2/1 LPC, P2, *P1, K4, P3*.

**Row 46:** *K3, P4, K1*, (K2, P2) two times, K3, P4, (K4, P3) two times, K5, P6, K5, (P3, K4) two times, P4, K3, (P2, K2) two times, *K1, P4, K3*.

**Row 47:** *P3, 2/2 RC, P1*, (P2, K2) two times, P3, 2/2 RC, (P4, K3) two times, P5, K6, P5, (K3, P4) two times, 2/2 RC, P3, (K2, P2) two times, *P1, 2/2 RC, P3*.

**Row 48:** *K3, P4, K1*, (K2, P2) two times, K3, P4, (K4, P3) two times, K5, P6, K5, (P3, K4) two times, P4, K3, (P2, K2) two times, *K1, P4, K3*.

## 2x2 Elastic Bind Off (for 2x2 Rib with Selvage, flat over a multiple of 4 sts)

**On RS:** K1, *(Sl st from RH needle to LH needle, K2tog TBL) two times, (P1, pass st from RH needle over) two times, rep from * to last 3 sts, (Sl st from RH needle to LH needle, K2tog TBL) two times, P1, pass st from RH needle over, break working yarn and pull it through final st to complete BO.

## 2x2 Elastic Bind Off (for 2x2 Rib, in the round over a multiple of 4 sts)

K1, *(P1, pass st from RH needle over) two times, (Sl st from RH needle to LH needle, K2tog TBL) two times, rep from * to last 3 sts, (P1, pass st from RH needle over) two times, Sl st from RH needle to LH needle, K2tog TBL, break working yarn and pull it through both first and final st to complete BO and seal the rnd.

# DIRECTIONS

Sts between * * are only worked for sizes 46–56" & 58–68".

## Long Rectangle

### Edging

With smaller longer needles, CO 100 (140, 188, 228) sts using Long Tail Cast On.

Work 2x2 Rib with Selvage for nine rows.

### Transition

Switch to larger needles.

**Row 1 (RS):** Sl1, RT, P2, 2/1 LPC, 2/1 RPC, P2, K1, M1L, K1, P2, SSK, (P2, K2) two times, P2, K2tog, P2, K1, M1L, K1, (P2, 2/1 LPC, 2/1 RPC) two times, (P2, K2) two times, *P2, 2/1 LPC, 2/1 RPC*, P1, M1L, P1, RT, PM, P2tog, (K2tog, P1, K1, P1) 6 (14, 22, 30) times, K2tog, RT, K1. 93 (125, 165, 197) sts.

**Row 2 (WS):** Sl1, P2, (K1, P1) to M, SM, P2, *K4, P4*, K3, P2, K2, P2, K3, P4, K4, P4, K3, P3, K5, P6, K5, P3, K3, P4, K3, P3.

### Body

**Row 1 (RS):** Work Long Rectangle Chart to M, SM, (K1, P1) to last 3 sts, RT, K1.

**Row 2 (WS):** Sl1, P2, (P1, K1) to M, SM, work Long Rectangle Chart.

**Row 3:** Work Long Rectangle Chart to M, SM, (P1, K1) to last 3 sts, RT, K1.

**Row 4:** Sl1, P2, (K1, P1) to M, SM, work Long Rectangle Chart. Rep Rows 1–4 until all rows of chart have been worked 5 (7, 9, 11) times, then cont to work Rows 1–25 of chart once more.

## Transition

**Row 1 (WS):** Sl1, P2, (P1, K1) to M, SM, P2, *K4, P4*, K3, P2, K2, P2, K3, P4, K4, P4, K3, P3, K5, P6, K5, P3, K3, P4, K3, P3.
**Row 2 (RS):** Sl1, RT, P2, 2/1 RPC, 2/1 LPC, P2, K1, K2tog, P2, M1L, K1, (P2, K2) two times, P2, K1, M1L, P2, SSK, K1, (P2, 2/1 RPC, 2/1 LPC) two times, (P2, K2) two times, *P2, 2/1 RPC, 2/1 LPC*, P1, P2tog, RT, remove M, M1P, P1, (M1L, K1, P2, K1, M1L, P2, K2, M1P, P1, K2, P1, M1P, K2, P2) 1 (3, 5, 7) times, M1L, K1, P2, K1, M1L, P2, K2, M1P, P1, RT, K1. 100 (140, 188, 228) sts.

## Edging

Switch to smaller longer needles.
Work 2x2 Rib with Selvage for nine rows.
BO using 2x2 Elastic Bind Off.

## Side Panel

### Edging

Fold Long Rectangle in half with RS facing outwards. Side Panel joins it along Moss Stitch side and is worked starting from 2x2 Rib up to neckline.
With smaller longer needles, CO 76 (76, 92, 92) sts using Long Tail Cast On. Pull tail through last st at RH corner of BO row of Long Rectangle and secure it. Turn to WS.
**Row 1 (WS):** Sl1, (K2, P2) to last 3 sts, K2, PU first selvage st of Long Rectangle at its Moss Stitch CO side and P2tog with last st on LH needle. Turn to RS.
**Row 2 (RS):** Sl1, (P2, K2) to last 3 sts, P2, PU second selvage st of Long Rectangle at its Moss Stitch BO side and K2tog with last st on LH needle. Turn to WS.
Cont as established for nine rows total.

### Transition

Switch to larger needles.
**Row 1 (RS):** Sl1, *P2, 2/1 LPC, 2/1 RPC*, (P2, K2) two times, (P2, 2/1 LPC, 2/1 RPC) two times, P2, K1, M1L, K1, P2, SSK, (P2, K2) two times, P2, K2tog, P2, K1, M1L, K1, (P2, 2/1 LPC, 2/1 RPC) two times, (P2, K2) two times, P2, *2/1 LPC, 2/1 RPC, P2*, PU corresponding selvage st of Long Rectangle at its Moss Stitch BO side and K2tog with last st on LH needle. Turn to WS.
**Row 2 (WS):** Sl1, *K3, P4, K1*, (K2, P2) two times, K3, P4, K4, P4, K3, P3, K5, P6, K5, P3, K3, P4, K4, P4, K3, (P2, K2) two times, *K1, P4, K3*, PU corresponding selvage st of Long Rectangle at its Moss Stitch CO side and P2tog with last st on LH needle. Turn to RS.

### Body

**Row 1 (RS):** Sl1, work Side Panel Chart to last st, PU corresponding selvage st of Long Rectangle at its Moss Stitch BO side and K2tog with last st on LH needle. Turn to WS.
**Row 2 (WS):** Sl1, work Side Panel Chart to last st, PU corresponding selvage st of Long Rectangle at its Moss Stitch CO side and P2tog with last st on LH needle. Turn to RS.
Rep Rows 1–2 until all rows of chart have been worked 1 (2, 3, 4) times, then cont to work Rows 1–43 (43, 35, 35) of chart once more.

## Transition

### Sizes 32″ & 34–44″ Only

**Row 1 (WS):** Sl1, K3, (P4, K4) two times, P4, K3, P3, K5, P6, K5, P3, K3, (P4, K4) two times, P4, K3, PU corresponding selvage st of Long Rectangle at its Moss Stitch CO side and P2tog with last st on LH needle. Turn to RS.
**Row 2 (RS):** Sl1, (P2, 2/1 RPC, 2/1 LPC) three times, P2, K1, K2tog, P2, M1L, K1, (P2, K2) two times, P2, K1, M1L, P2, SSK, K1, (P2, 2/1 RPC, 2/1 LPC) three times, P2, PU corresponding selvage st of Long Rectangle at its Moss Stitch BO side and K2tog with last st on LH needle.

### Sizes 46–56″ & 58–68″ Only

**Row 1 (WS):** Sl1, (K2, P2) two times, K3, P4, K3, P2, K2, P2, K5, P6, K5, P3, K4, P3, K5, P6, K5, P2, K2, P2, K3, P4, K3, (P2, K2) two times, PU corresponding selvage st of Long Rectangle at its Moss Stitch CO side and P2tog with last st on LH needle. Turn to RS.
**Row 2 (RS):** Sl1, (P2, K2) two times, P2, 2/1 RPC, 2/1 LPC, (P2, K2) two times, P2, K1, M1L, (P2, K2) three times, P1, 2/1 LPC, (P2tog) two times, 2/1 RPC, P1, (K2, P2) three times, K1, M1L, (P2, K2) two times, P2, 2/1 RPC, 2/1 LPC, (P2, K2) two times, P2, PU corresponding selvage st of Long Rectangle at its Moss Stitch BO side and K2tog with last st on LH needle.

## Neckline (resume all sizes)

Transfer all 76 (76, 92, 92) sts of Side Panel to smaller circular needles (16″). PM at end of row. With same needles, along edge of Long Rectangle, PU 76 (76, 92, 92) sts and K1, (P2, K2) to last 3 sts, P2, K1.
Join to work in the rnd; PM for BOR. 152 (152, 184, 184) sts.
**Rnd 1:** *SSK, P1, (K2, P2) to last 5 sts before M, K2, P1, K2tog, SM; rep from * once more. 148 (148, 180, 180) sts.
**Rnd 2:** *K1, P1, (K2, P2) to last 4 sts before M, K2, P1, K1, SM; rep from * once more.
**Rnd 3:** *SSK, (K2, P2) to last 4 sts before M, K2, K2tog, SM; rep from * once more. 144 (144, 176, 176) sts.
**Rnd 4:** *K1, (K2, P2) to last 3 sts before M, K3, SM; rep from * once more.
**Rnd 5:** *SSK, K1, (P2, K2) to last 5 sts before M, P2, K1, K2tog, SM; rep from * once more. 140 (140, 172, 172) sts.
**Rnd 6:** *(K2, P2) to last 2 sts before M, K2, SM; rep from * once more.
**Rnd 7:** *SSK, (P2, K2) to last 4 sts before M, P2, K2tog, SM; rep from * once more. 136 (136, 168, 168) sts.
BO using 2x2 Elastic Bind Off.

## Finishing

Weave in ends, wash, and block to open up cables.

## LEGEND

**K**
RS: Knit stitch
WS: Purl stitch

● **P**
RS: Purl stitch
WS: Knit stitch

∨ **Sl**
Slip stitch purl-wise,
with yarn in back

☐ **Work for Sizes 46-56"
& 58-68" Only**

**Right Twist (RT)**
Sl1 to CN, hold in back; K1, K1 from CN

**Cable 2 Over 1 Right, Purl back (2/1 RPC)**
Sl1 to CN, hold in back; K2, P1 from CN

**Cable 2 Over 1 Left, Purl back (2/1 LPC)**
Sl2 to CN, hold in front; P1, K2 from CN

**Cable 2 Over 2 Right (2/2 RC)**
Sl2 to CN, hold in back; K2, K2 from CN

**Cable 3 Over 1 Right, Purl back (3/1 RPC)**
Sl1 to CN, hold in back; K3, P1 from CN

**Cable 3 Over 1 Left, Purl back (3/1 LPC)**
Sl3 to CN, hold in front; P1, K3 from CN

**Cable 3 Over 2 Right, Purl back (3/2 RPC)**
Sl2 to CN, hold in back; K3, P2 from CN

**Cable 3 Over 2 Left, Purl back (3/2 LPC)**
Sl3 to CN, hold in front; P2, K3 from CN

**Cable 3 Over 3 Right (3/3 RC)**
Sl3 to CN, hold in back; K3, K3 from CN

**Cable 3 Over 3 Left (3/3 LC)**
Sl3 to CN, hold in front; K3, K3 from CN

## Long Rectangle Chart

## Side Panel Chart

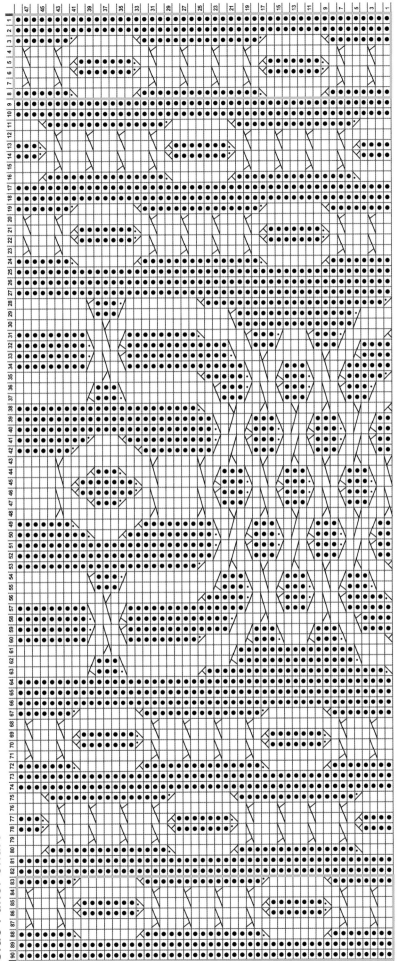

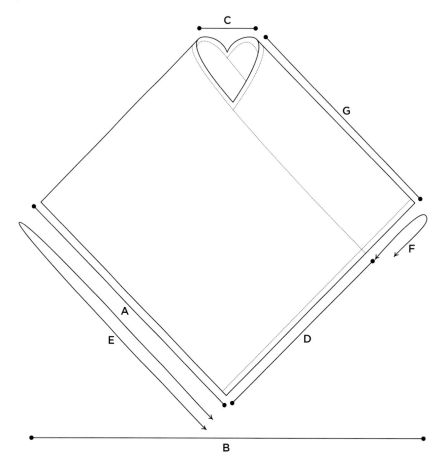

**A** *length along edge* 21 (28, 35, 42.25)"
**B** *total width* 30.25 (39.5, 49.5, 59.75)"
**C** *neck width* 7.25 (7.25, 9, 9)"
**D** *long rectangle CO edge* 15.75 (22, 29.5, 36)"
**E** *long rectangle total length* 41.75 (58.25, 69.75, 83.5)"
**F** *side panel CO edge* 12 (12, 14.5, 14.5)"
**G** *side panel length* 16.25 (23, 29, 35)"

# DIAMONDS ARE FOR EVERYONE

by Holli Yeoh

## FINISHED MEASUREMENTS

38 (39.75, 42.75, 46.5, 50.25, 54.5)(57.75, 62.5, 65.75, 70.25, 73.75)" finished chest circumference, meant to be worn with approx 5" positive ease
*Sample is 39.75" size; model is 31" chest*

## YARN

Twill™ (worsted weight, 100% Superwash Merino Wool; 149 yards/100g): Gold Rush 27934, 13 (13, 15, 16, 17, 19)(20, 22, 24, 26, 27) hanks

## NEEDLES

US 6 (4mm) straight or 24" or longer circular needles, or size to obtain gauge

US 5 (3.75mm) straight or 24" or longer circular needles, or one size smaller than size used to obtain gauge
US 5 (3.75mm) 16" circular needles, or one size smaller than size used to obtain gauge

## NOTIONS

Yarn Needle
Stitch Markers
Locking Stitch Markers
Cable Needle

## GAUGE

17.5 sts and 27 rows = 4" in Stockinette Stitch, blocked
25 sts and 28 rows = 4" in Diamond pattern, blocked

For pattern support, contact info@holliyeoh.com

# Diamonds Are for Everyone

*Notes:*

Richly textured geometric patterning and a unisex fit make for a truly timeless pullover. The firm, strongly defined lines of twisted stitches form tiled layers across the body and run down the sleeves in a single line, grounded with smooth stocking stitch.

The pullover is worked bottom up in pieces, with an inclusive range of eleven sizes that takes into account the proportions of the twisted stitch diamond motif. Saddle shoulders ensure a perfect structure and flattering fit. Notes for simple modifications are included.

Stitch markers placed between pattern repeats are highly recommended. They are especially useful for keeping track of the twisted purl sts and, during the second half of the pattern repeat rows, the knit stitches on the WS are easier to locate in relation to the markers.

There are two Diamond Patterns (18-st and 22-st), each proportionally sized for different size ranges. Use the appropriate stitch pattern for your chosen size.

When shaping in pattern, if a twisted stitch cannot be completed, work the stitches in Stockinette Stitch. Always work selvage stitches in Stockinette Stitch.

Charts are worked flat; read RS rows (odd numbers) from right to left, and WS rows (even numbers) from left to right.

## Modification Notes

Sweater measurements are based on unisex sizing. To change the length of the pullover, work fewer or more rows before the underarm bind off on both Front and Back. For a more cropped effect, consider working 2–4″ less for body length from hem to underarm on both Front and Back.

To change the length of the sleeves, add or subtract length in the space between the top of the sleeve shaping and the underarm bind off.

To change the sleeve circumference, find the sleeve size that suits your needs and knit that size to the sleeve cap. Determine the difference in stitches (A) between the size you've knit and the original size. Divide A by 2 (B). Follow the original size sleeve cap, but for the first B Dec rows, work an extra decrease. i.e. If the Dec row is worked with double decreases, work triple decreases at each end.

For example, if working a 57.75″ size sweater with 62.5″ size sleeves, the total sleeve width difference is 6 sts (99 sts − 93 sts = 6 sts = A). Work the first 3 Dec rows (6 sts ÷ 2 = 3 Dec rows = B) with an extra decrease at each end of the row. The first row should have a double decrease so work a triple decrease. The next 2 Dec rows should be single decreases, so work them as double decreases. Work the remaining decreases as instructed for your original size.

If your row gauge is wildly different than the pattern gauge, the sleeve cap won't fit the armhole. Measure your row gauge to determine how many rows per inch for your gauge. Multiply the sleeve cap height (from the schematic) by the pattern row gauge (A). Multiply sleeve cap height by your row gauge (B). Subtract B from A (A − B = C) to get the number of rows you need to add or subtract from your sleeve cap; round this to an even number. If you need to subtract rows, take them from the section where you work the Dec row every fourth row. If you need to add rows, add them in the section where the Dec rows are worked every second row. The key is to keep the sleeve cap the same depth as the original pattern.

## K2tog Twisted Stitches

Twisted stitches (or 1-over-1 cables) are easier to work as K2tog twisted sts, but alternatively may be worked like normal cables. Instructions for both are included below. More methods can also be found here: knitpicks.com /learning-center/cabling-without-cable-needle.

### LT (Left Twist, with a cable needle)
Sl1 to CN, hold in front; K1, K1 from CN.

### LT (Left Twist, without a cable needle)
With RH needle, reach behind next st on needle and K into second st TBL, leaving st on LH needle, then K2tog TBL, sliding both sts off needle.

### RT (Right Twist, with a cable needle)
Sl1 to CN, hold in back; K1, K1 from CN.

### RT (Right Twist, without a cable needle)
K2tog leaving both sts on LH needle, then K into first st on needle, sliding both sts off LH needle.

### RLI (Right Lifted Increase)
With RH needle, K into right shoulder of st in row directly below the next st on LH needle. 1 st inc.

### LLI (Left Lifted Increase)
Use LH needle to pick up st 2 rows directly below last st worked and K into it. 1 st inc.

### GSR (German Short Row)
The short rows in this pattern are designed for the German Short Row method (see Glossary). When pattern says to turn, work German Short Row steps.

## Diamond Pattern
Use the right Diamond Pattern (18-st or 22-st) for your size.

### Sizes 38 (39.75, 42.75, 46.5, 50.25, -)(-, -, -, -, -)″
**18-st Diamond Pattern (flat over a multiple of 18 sts plus 17)**
Row 1 (RS): (LT) four times, K1 TBL, *(RT) four times, K1 TBL, (LT) four times, K1 TBL; rep from *, (RT) four times.
Row 2 (WS): P8, *(P1 TBL, P8) two times; rep from *, P1 TBL, P8.
Row 3: K1, (LT) three times, P1, K1 TBL, *P1, (RT) three times, P1, K1 TBL, P1, (LT) three times, P1, K1 TBL; rep from *, P1, (RT) three times, K1.

**Row 4:** P7, K1, *(P1 TBL, K1, P6, K1) two times; rep from *, P1 TBL, K1, P7.

**Row 5:** K2, (LT) three times, K1 TBL, *(RT) four times, K1 TBL, (LT) four times, K1 TBL; rep from *, (RT) three times, K2.

**Row 6:** Rep Row 2.

**Row 7:** K3, (LT) two times, P1, K1 TBL, *P1, (RT) three times, P1, K1 TBL, P1, (LT) three times, P1, K1 TBL; rep from *, P1, (RT) two times, K3.

**Row 8:** Rep Row 4.

**Row 9:** K4, (LT) two times, K1 TBL, *(RT) four times, K1 TBL, (LT) four times, K1 TBL; rep from *, (RT) two times, K4.

**Row 10:** Rep Row 2.

**Row 11:** K5, LT, P1, K1 TBL, *P1, (RT) three times, P1, K1 TBL, P1, (LT) three times, P1, K1 TBL; rep from *, P1, RT, K5.

**Row 12:** Rep Row 4.

**Row 13:** K6, LT, K1 TBL, *(RT) four times, K1 TBL, (LT) four times, K1 TBL; rep from *, RT, K6.

**Row 14:** Rep Row 2.

**Row 15:** K6, RT, K1 TBL, *LT, P1, (RT) two times, P1, K1 TBL, P1, (LT) two times, P1, RT, K1 TBL; rep from *, LT, K6.

**Row 16:** P8, *P1 TBL, P2, K1, P4, K1, P1 TBL, K1, P4, K1, P2; rep from *, P1 TBL, P8.

**Row 17:** K5, RT, P1, K1 TBL, *P1, LT, P1, (RT) two times, K1 TBL, (LT) two times, P1, RT, P1, K1 TBL; rep from *, P1, LT, K5.

**Row 18:** P7, K1, *P1 TBL, K1, P2, K1, P4, P1 TBL, P4, K1, P2, K1; rep from *, P1 TBL, K1, P7.

**Row 19:** K4, (RT) two times, K1 TBL, *(LT) two times, P1, RT, P1, K1 TBL, P1, LT, P1, (RT) two times, K1 TBL; rep from *, (LT) two times, K4.

**Row 20:** P8, *P1 TBL, P4, K1, P2, K1, P1 TBL, K1, P2, K1, P4; rep from *, P1 TBL, P8.

**Row 21:** K3, (RT) two times, P1, K1 TBL, *P1, (LT) two times, P1, RT, K1 TBL, LT, P1, (RT) two times, P1, K1 TBL; rep from *, P1, (LT) two times, K3.

**Row 22:** P7, K1, *P1 TBL, K1, P4, K1, P2, P1 TBL, P2, K1, P4, K1; rep from *, P1 TBL, K1, P7.

**Row 23:** K2, (RT) three times, K1 TBL, *(LT) three times, P2, K1 TBL, P2, (RT) three times, K1 TBL; rep from *, (LT) three times, K2.

**Row 24:** P8, *P1 TBL, P6, K2, P1 TBL, K2, P6; rep from *, P1 TBL, P8.

**Row 25:** K1, (RT) three times, P1, K1 TBL, *P1, (LT) three times, P1, K1 TBL, P1, (RT) three times, P1, K1 TBL; rep from *, P1, (LT) three times, K1.

**Row 26:** Rep Row 4.

**Row 27:** (RT) four times, K1 TBL, *(LT) four times, K1 TBL, (RT) four times, K1 TBL; rep from *, (LT) four times.

**Row 28:** Rep Row 2.

**Sizes - (-, -, -, -, 54.5)(57.75, 62.5, 65.75, 70.25, 73.75)"**
**22-st Diamond Pattern (flat over a multiple of 22 sts plus 21)**

**Row 1 (RS):** (LT) five times, K1 TBL, *(RT) five times, K1 TBL, (LT) five times, K1 TBL; rep from *, (RT) five times.

**Row 2 (WS):** P10, *(P1 TBL, P10) two times; rep from *, P1 TBL, P10.

**Row 3:** K1, (LT) four times, P1, K1 TBL, *P1, (RT) four times, P1, K1 TBL, P1, (LT) four times, P1, K1 TBL; rep from *, P1, (RT) four times, K1.

**Row 4:** P9, K1, *(P1 TBL, K1, P8, K1) two times; rep from *, P1 TBL, K1, P9.

**Row 5:** K2, (LT) four times, K1 TBL, *(RT) five times, K1 TBL, (LT) five times, K1 TBL; rep from *, (RT) four times, K2.

**Row 6:** Rep Row 2.

**Row 7:** K3, (LT) three times, P1, K1 TBL, *P1, (RT) four times, P1, K1 TBL, P1, (LT) four times, P1, K1 TBL; rep from *, P1, (RT) three times, K3.

**Row 8:** Rep Row 4.

**Row 9:** K4, (LT) three times, K1 TBL, *(RT) five times, K1 TBL, (LT) five times, K1 TBL; rep from *, (RT) three times, K4.

**Row 10:** Rep Row 2.

**Row 11:** K5, (LT) two times, P1, K1 TBL, *P1, (RT) four times, P1, K1 TBL, P1, (LT) four times, P1, K1 TBL; rep from *, P1, (RT) two times, K5.

**Row 12:** Rep Row 4.

**Row 13:** K6, (LT) two times, K1 TBL, *(RT) five times, K1 TBL, (LT) five times, K1 TBL; rep from *, (RT) two times, K6.

**Row 14:** Rep Row 2.

**Row 15:** K7, LT, P1, K1 TBL, *P1, (RT) four times, P1, K1 TBL, P1, (LT) four times, P1, K1 TBL; rep from *, P1, RT, K7.

**Row 16:** Rep Row 4.

**Row 17:** K8, LT, K1 TBL, *(RT) five times, K1 TBL, (LT) five times, K1 TBL; rep from *, RT, K8.

**Row 18:** Rep Row 2.

**Row 19:** K8, RT, K1 TBL, *LT, P1, (RT) three times, P1, K1 TBL, P1, (LT) three times, P1, RT, K1 TBL; rep from *, LT, K8.

**Row 20:** P10, *P1 TBL, P2, K1, P6, K1, P1 TBL, K1, P6, K1, P2; rep from *, P1 TBL, P10.

**Row 21:** K7, RT, P1, K1 TBL, *P1, LT, P1, (RT) three times, K1 TBL, (LT) three times, P1, RT, P1, K1 TBL; rep from *, P1, LT, K7.

**Row 22:** P9, K1, *P1 TBL, K1, P2, K1, P6, P1 TBL, P6, K1, P2, K1; rep from *, P1 TBL, K1, P9.

**Row 23:** K6, (RT) two times, K1 TBL, *(LT) two times, P1, (RT) two times, P1, K1 TBL, P1, (LT) two times, P1, (RT) two times, K1 TBL; rep from *, (LT) two times, K6.

**Row 24:** P10, *P1 TBL, (P4, K1) two times, P1 TBL, (K1, P4) two times; rep from *, P1 TBL, P10.

**Row 25:** K5, (RT) two times, P1, K1 TBL, *P1, (LT) two times, P1, (RT) two times, K1 TBL, (LT) two times, P1, (RT) two times, P1, K1 TBL; rep from *, P1, (LT) two times, K5.

**Row 26:** P9, K1, *P1 TBL, (K1, P4) two times, P1 TBL, (P4, K1) two times; rep from *, P1 TBL, K1, P9.

**Row 27:** K4, (RT) three times, K1 TBL, *(LT) three times, P1, RT, P1, K1 TBL, P1, LT, P1, (RT) three times, K1 TBL; rep from *, (LT) three times, K4.

**Row 28:** P10, *P1 TBL, P6, K1, P2, K1, P1 TBL, K1, P2, K1, P6; rep from *, P1 TBL, P10.

**Row 29:** K3, (RT) three times, P1, K1 TBL, *P1, (LT) three times, P1, RT, K1 TBL, LT, P1, (RT) three times, P1, K1 TBL; rep from *, P1, (LT) three times, K3.

**Row 30:** P9, K1, *P1 TBL, K1, P6, K1, P2, P1 TBL, P2, K1, P6, K1; rep from *, P1 TBL, K1, P9.

**Row 31:** K2, (RT) four times, K1 TBL, *(LT) four times, P2, K1 TBL, P2, (RT) four times, K1 TBL; rep from *, (LT) four times, K2.

**Row 32:** P10, *P1 TBL, P8, K2, P1 TBL, K2, P8; rep from *, P1 TBL, P10.

**Row 33:** K1, (RT) four times, P1, K1 TBL, *P1, (LT) four times, P1, K1 TBL, P1, (RT) four times, P1, K1 TBL; rep from *, P1, (LT) four times, K1.

**Row 34:** Rep Row 4.

**Row 35:** (RT) five times, K1 TBL, *(LT) five times, K1 TBL, (RT) five times, K1 TBL; rep from *, (LT) five times.

**Row 36:** Rep Row 2.

## DIRECTIONS

### Back

#### Ribbing

With smaller needles, CO 120 (124, 134, 142, 156, 168)(184, 192, 206, 216, 232) sts.

**Row 1 (RS):** K1, (K1, P1) to last st, K1.

**Row 2 (WS):** (P1, K1) to last 2 sts, P2.

Work 1x1 Rib as established for 11 more rows.

**Dec Row (WS):** P1, K1, (P2tog) 1 (1, 0, 0, 0, 0)(1, 0, 0, 0, 1) time(s), work Rib pattern to last 6 sts, (P2tog) 2 (2, 1, 1, 1, 1)(2, 1, 1, 1, 2) time(s), work in pattern to end. 117 (121, 133, 141, 155, 167)(181, 191, 205, 215, 229) sts.

#### Body

Diamond Pattern begins on next row—select appropriate Diamond Pattern for size being made.

Change to larger needles.

**Row 1 (RS):** K5 (7, 4, 8, 6, 7)(3, 8, 4, 9, 5), beginning with Row 1 of appropriate Diamond Pattern, work chart to last 5 (7, 4, 8, 6, 7)(3, 8, 4, 9, 5) sts, K to end.

**Row 2 (WS):** P5 (7, 4, 8, 6, 7)(3, 8, 4, 9, 5), work next row of Diamond Pattern to last 5 (7, 4, 8, 6, 7)(3, 8, 4, 9, 5) sts, P to end.

Work Diamond Pattern with edge sts as established (in St st) until piece measures 13.5 (13.5, 14, 14, 14, 13.5)(13.5, 13.5, 13.5, 13.5, 13.5)" from CO edge, ending with a WS row.

#### Armhole Shaping

Maintain Diamond Pattern throughout armhole shaping. (See note on working shaping in pattern.)

BO 5 (6, 8, 8, 10, 10)(12, 11, 13, 12, 15) sts at beginning of next two rows, working rest of row in Diamond Pattern. 107 (109, 117, 125, 135, 147)(157, 169, 179, 191, 199) sts remain.

#### Sizes - (-, -, -, -, 54.5)(57.75, 62.5, 65.75, 70.25, 73.75)" Only

**Double Dec Row (RS):** K1, K3tog, work in pattern to last 4 sts, SSSK, K1. 4 sts dec.

Rep Double Dec Row every RS row - (-, -, -, -, 0)(0, 1, 2, 3, 4) more time(s). - (-, -, -, -, 143)(153, 161, 167, 175, 179) sts remain.

#### Resume All Sizes

**Dec Row (RS):** K1, K2tog, work in pattern to last 3 sts, SSK, K1. 2 sts dec.

Rep Dec Row every RS row 5 (6, 8, 10, 12, 13)(15, 17, 17, 19, 19) more times. 95 (95, 99, 103, 109, 115)(121, 125, 131, 135, 139) sts remain.

Working first and last st of every row in St st, WE in pattern

until armhole measures 7.5 (8, 8, 8.5, 9, 9.25)(9.75, 10.25, 10.75, 11.25, 11.75)" from underarm BO, ending with a WS row.

#### Shoulder & Neck Shaping

Shoulders are shaped with short rows and worked in Diamond Pattern throughout. The German Short Row method (see Notes) is recommended.

Ms are placed throughout short row shaping to make it easier to work them. When instructed to work a specific number of sts at beginning of short row after turn, count GSR "double stitch" as first st.

Sometimes Ms need to be placed between the 2 sts in a twisted st. To do this, work first st of LT or RT, PM, then work second st.

**Short Row 1 (RS):** Work to last 4 (4, 4, 4, 4, 5)(5, 5, 5, 5, 5) sts, turn (work GSR).

**Short Row 2 (WS):** Work 4 (4, 4, 4, 4, 4)(5, 5, 5, 5, 5) sts, PM, work to last 4 (4, 4, 4, 4, 5)(5, 5, 5, 5, 5) sts, turn.

**Short Rows 3–5:** Work 4 (4, 4, 4, 4, 4)(5, 5, 5, 5, 5), PM, work to next M, turn.

**Short Rows 6–9:** Work 3 (3, 3, 3, 4, 4)(4, 4, 5, 5, 5), PM, work to next M, turn.

**Short Rows 10–11:** Work 3 (3, 3, 3, 3, 4)(4, 4, 4, 5, 5), PM, work to next M, turn.

**Short Rows 12–13:** Work 3 (3, 3, 3, 3, 4)(4, 4, 4, 4, 5), PM, work to next M, turn.

**Short Row 14:** Work to next M, turn.

*Note:* Double sts from GSR appear immediately before Ms in next two rows and are worked tog as if 1 st.

**Next Row (RS):** Work to next M, SM, K to end of row, removing remaining Ms as you go. 24 (24, 24, 24, 26, 29)(31, 31, 33, 34, 35) sts between slipped M and end of row.

**Next Row (WS):** BO 24 (24, 24, 24, 26, 29)(31, 31, 33, 34, 35) sts P-wise, place locking M (optional) to mark neck opening, work in pattern to next M, SM, P to end of row, removing Ms. 71 (71, 75, 79, 83, 86)(90, 94, 98, 101, 104) sts remain; 47 (47, 51, 55, 57, 57)(59, 63, 65, 67, 69) neck sts; 24 (24, 24, 24, 26, 29)(31, 31, 33, 34, 35) shoulder sts.

**Next Row:** BO 24 (24, 24, 24, 26, 29)(31, 31, 33, 34, 35) sts, place locking M (optional) to mark neck opening, BO remaining sts.

### Front

Work as for Back until armhole measures 7.25 (7.75, 7.5, 7.75, 8.25, 8.5)(9.25, 9.25, 9.75, 10.25, 10.75)" from underarm BO, ending with a WS row. 95 (95, 99, 103, 109, 115)(121, 125, 131, 135, 139) sts remain.

#### Left Neck Shaping

**Row 1 (RS):** Work 35 (35, 36, 37, 39, 42)(45, 46, 48, 50, 51) sts in pattern, Sl1. Cont on this set of sts only for left neckline and shoulder shaping.

**Row 2 (WS):** Sl2, pass first st over second st, BO 2 sts P-wise, work to end of row. 3 sts dec; 33 (33, 34, 35, 37, 40)(43, 44, 46, 48, 49) sts remain.

**Row 3:** Work to last st, Sl1.

Rep Rows 2–3 another 0 (0, 1, 1, 1, 1)(1, 2, 2, 2, 2) time(s). 33 (33, 31, 32, 34, 37)(40, 38, 40, 42, 43) sts.

## Left Neck & Shoulder Shaping

**Short Row 1 (WS):** Sl2, pass first st over second st, BO 2 (2, 1, 1, 1, 1)(2, 1, 1, 1, 1) st(s) P-wise, work to last 4 (4, 4, 4, 4, 5)(5, 5, 5, 5, 5) sts, turn (work GSR). 3 (3, 2, 2, 2, 2)(3, 2, 2, 2, 2) sts dec.

**Short Row 2 (RS):** Work 4 (4, 4, 4, 4, 4)(5, 5, 5, 5, 5) sts, PM, work to last st, Sl1.

**Short Row 3:** Sl2, pass first st over second st, BO 1 st P-wise, work to M, turn. 2 st dec.

**Short Row 4:** Work 4 (4, 4, 4, 4, 4)(5, 5, 5, 5, 5) sts, PM, work to last st, Sl1.

**Short Row 5:** Sl2, pass first st over second st, BO 1 (1, 0, 1, 1, 1)(1, 0, 0, 1, 1) st(s) P-wise, work to M, turn. 2 (2, 1, 2, 2, 2)(2, 1, 1, 2, 2) st(s) dec.

**Short Row 6:** Work 3 (3, 3, 3, 4, 4)(4, 4, 5, 5, 5) sts, PM, work to last st, Sl1.

**Short Row 7:** Sl2, pass first st over second st, work to M, turn. 1 st dec.

**Short Row 8:** Rep Short Row 6.

**Short Row 9:** Sl2, pass first st over second st, work to M, turn. 1 st dec.

**Short Row 10:** Work 3 (3, 3, 3, 3, 4)(4, 4, 4, 5, 5) sts, PM, work to end (don't Sl last st).

**Short Row 11:** Work to M, turn.

**Short Row 12:** WE in pattern.

*Note:* Double sts from GSR appear immediately before Ms in next row and are worked tog as if 1 st.

**Row 13:** Removing Ms as you go, P across. 24 (24, 24, 24, 26, 29)(31, 31, 33, 34, 35) sts.

BO all left shoulder sts.

## Right Neck Shaping

**Row 1 (RS):** Rejoin yarn at center front and BO 23 (23, 25, 27, 29, 29)(29, 31, 33, 33, 35) sts, work in pattern to end of row. 36 (36, 37, 38, 40, 43)(46, 47, 49, 51, 52) sts remain.

**Row 2 (WS):** Work to last st, Sl1.

**Row 3:** Sl2, pass first st over second st, BO 2 sts, work in pattern to end of row. 3 sts dec; 33 (33, 34, 35, 37, 40)(43, 44, 46, 48, 49) sts remain.

**Row 4:** Rep Row 2.

Rep Rows 3–4 another 0 (0, 1, 1, 1, 1)(1, 2, 2, 2, 2) time(s). 33 (33, 31, 32, 34, 37)(40, 38, 40, 42, 43) sts.

## Right Neck & Shoulder Shaping

**Short Row 1 (RS):** Sl2, pass first st over second st, BO 2 (2, 1, 1, 1, 1)(2, 1, 1, 1, 1) st(s), work to last 4 (4, 4, 4, 4, 5)(5, 5, 5, 5, 5) sts, turn (work GSR). 3 (3, 2, 2, 2, 2)(3, 2, 2, 2, 2) sts dec.

**Short Row 2 (WS):** Work 4 (4, 4, 4, 4, 4)(5, 5, 5, 5, 5) sts, PM, work to last st, Sl1.

**Short Row 3:** Sl2, pass first st over second st, BO 1 st, work to M, turn. 2 sts dec.

**Short Row 4:** Work 4 (4, 4, 4, 4, 4)(5, 5, 5, 5, 5) sts, PM, work to last st, Sl1.

**Short Row 5:** Sl2, pass first st over second st, BO 1 (1, 0, 1, 1, 1)(1, 0, 0, 1, 1) st, work to M, turn. 2 (2, 1, 2, 2, 2)(2, 1, 1, 2, 2) st(s) dec.

**Short Row 6:** Work 3 (3, 3, 3, 4, 4)(4, 4, 5, 5, 5) sts, PM, work to last st, Sl1.

**Short Row 7:** Sl2, pass first st over second st, work to M, turn. 1 st dec.

**Short Row 8:** Rep Short Row 6.

**Short Row 9:** Sl2, pass first st over second st, work to M, turn. 1 st dec.

**Short Row 10:** Work 3 (3, 3, 3, 3, 4)(4, 4, 5, 5) sts, PM, work to end (don't Sl last st).

**Short Row 11:** Work to M, turn.

**Short Row 12:** WE in pattern.

*Note:* Double sts from GSR appear immediately before Ms in next row and are worked tog as if 1 st.

**Row 13:** Removing Ms as you go, K across. 24 (24, 24, 24, 26, 29)(31, 31, 33, 34, 35) sts.

BO all right shoulder sts.

## Sleeves (make two the same)

### Ribbing

With smaller needles, CO 44 (44, 46, 48, 48, 54)(54, 58, 58, 62, 62) sts.

**Row 1 (RS):** K0 (0, 1, 0, 0, 1)(1, 1, 1, 1, 1), (K1, P1) to last 2 (2, 1, 2, 2, 1)(1, 1, 1, 1, 1) st(s), K to end.

**Row 2 (WS):** P2 (2, 1, 2, 2, 1)(1, 1, 1, 1, 1), (K1, P1) to last 0 (0, 1, 0, 0, 1)(1, 1, 1, 1, 1) st(s), P to end.

Work 1x1 Rib as established for 13 more rows.

**Dec Row (WS):** P2 (2, 1, 2, 2, 1)(1, 1, 1, 1, 1), (K1, P1) to last 4 (4, 5, 4, 4, 5)(5, 5, 5, 5, 5) sts, K1, P2tog, P to end. 43 (43, 45, 47, 47, 53)(53, 57, 57, 61, 61) sts remain.

Begin working Diamond Pattern as follows.
Change to larger needles.
Use appropriate Diamond Pattern for size being made—the actual rep (as outlined in red on chart or between asterisks in written instructions) will not be worked. Only the 17 (17, 17, 17, 17, 21)(21, 21, 21, 21, 21) sts outside rep are worked on sleeve.

**Setup Row (RS):** K13 (13, 14, 15, 15, 16)(16, 18, 18, 20, 20), beginning with Row 1 work first 9 (9, 9, 9, 9, 11)(11, 11, 11, 11, 11) sts of Diamond Pattern, work last 8 (8, 8, 8, 8, 10)(10, 10, 10, 10, 10) sts of Diamond Pattern, K remaining 13 (13, 14, 15, 15, 16)(16, 18, 18, 20, 20) sts.

**Next Row (WS):** P13 (13, 14, 15, 15, 16)(16, 18, 18, 20, 20), work first 8 (8, 8, 8, 8, 10)(10, 10, 10, 10, 10) sts of next Diamond Pattern row (if working from chart, read row from left to right), work last 9 (9, 9, 9, 9, 11)(11, 11, 11, 11, 11) sts of Diamond Pattern, P remaining 13 (13, 14, 15, 15, 16)(16, 18, 18, 20, 20) sts.

Remainder of sleeve is worked in St st as established with Diamond Pattern in center of sleeve.

### Sleeve Shaping

**Inc Row (RS):** K2, RLI, work to last 2 sts, LLI, K2. 2 sts inc.

Working in pattern, rep Inc Row every 6 (4, 4, 4, 4, 4)(2, 2, 2, 2, 2) rows 12 (5, 4, 6, 13, 16)(3, 6, 12, 14, 19) more times. 69 (55, 55, 61, 75, 87)(61, 71, 83, 91, 101) sts.

Then rep Inc Row every 0 (6, 6, 6, 6, 6)(4, 4, 4, 4, 4) rows 0 (8, 9, 8, 3, 1)(16, 14, 11, 10, 7) time(s). 69 (71, 73, 77, 81, 89)(93, 99, 105, 111, 115) sts.

WE in pattern until piece measures 17 (16.25, 16.5, 16.75, 16.75, 16.5)(16.5, 16.25, 16.25, 16.25, 16.25)" from underarm CO, ending with a WS row.

## Sleeve Cap Shaping

BO 5 (6, 8, 8, 10, 10)(12, 11, 13, 12, 15) sts at beginning of next two rows. 59 (59, 57, 61, 61, 69)(69, 77, 79, 87, 85) sts.

**Single Dec Row (RS):** K1, K2tog, work to last 3 sts, SSK, K1. 2 sts dec.

Rep Single Dec Row every RS row 12 (10, 7, 10, 7, 11)(9, 16, 16, 23, 18) more time(s). 33 (37, 41, 39, 45, 45)(49, 43, 45, 39, 47) sts. Then rep Single Dec Row every four rows 1 (3, 5, 4, 7, 5)(7, 4, 5, 2, 6) time(s). 31 (31, 31, 31, 31, 35)(35, 35, 35, 35, 35) sts. Work one WS row.

**Double Dec Row (RS):** K1, K3tog, work in pattern to last 4 sts, SSSK, K1. 4 sts dec.

Work Double Dec Row every RS row two more times. 19 (19, 19, 19, 19, 23)(23, 23, 23, 23, 23) sts.

Work one WS row. Place Ms at each end of row to mark end of sleeve cap shaping and beginning of saddle.

WE in pattern until saddle measures 4 (4, 4, 4, 4.25, 4.5)(4.75, 4.75, 5, 5.25, 5.25)" from top of sleeve cap, ending with a WS row.

BO all sts.

## Finishing

Wash and gently block pieces to schematic measurements. Sew saddle shoulder seams matching Ms on sleeves to armhole edge of shoulders on both Front and Back. Sew sleeve caps into armholes, matching BO edges. Using Mattress Stitch, sew sleeve and side seams.

### Neckband

With RS facing, using smaller circular needles, PU and K: 17 (17, 17, 17, 17, 21)(21, 21, 21, 21, 21) sts along left saddle, 16 (16, 17, 18, 18, 18)(19, 20, 20, 21, 21) sts along left front neck from shoulder to center front BO, 23 (23, 25, 27, 29, 29)(29, 31, 33, 33, 35) sts along center front BO, 16 (16, 17, 18, 18, 18)(19, 20, 20, 21, 21) sts along right front neck to shoulder, 17 (17, 17, 17, 17, 21)(21, 21, 21, 21, 21) sts along right saddle, 49 (49, 53, 57, 59, 59)(61, 65, 67, 69, 71) sts along back neck. 138 (138, 146, 154, 158, 166)(170, 178, 182, 186, 190) sts. Join to work in the rnd.

**Rnd 1:** (K1, P1) to end.

Work 1x1 Rib until neckband measures 1".

BO in pattern.

### Final Finishing

Weave in ends.

## LEGEND

| | |
|---|---|
| ☐ | **K** RS: Knit stitch WS: Purl stitch |
| ⊡ | **P** RS: Purl stitch WS: Knit stitch |
| B | **K TBL** RS: Knit stitch through the back loop WS: Purl stitch through the back loop |
| ⧄⧅ | **Right Twist (RT)** Sl1 to CN, hold in back; K1, K1 from CN |
| ⧅⧄ | **Left Twist (LT)** Sl1 to CN, hold in front; K1, K1 from CN |
| ☐ | **Pattern Repeat** |

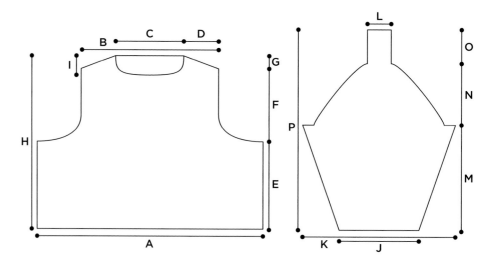

A *back/front width* 19.5 (20.25, 21.75, 23.75, 25.5, 27.75)(29.25, 31.75, 33.25, 35.75, 37.25)"

B *bodice width* 15.25 (15.25, 15.75, 16.5, 17.5, 18.5)(19.25, 20, 21, 21.5, 22.25)"

C *back neck* 7.5 (7.5, 8.25, 8.75, 9, 9)(9.5, 10, 10.5, 10.75, 11)"

D *shoulder width* 3.75 (3.75, 3.75, 3.75, 4.25, 4.75)(5, 5, 5.25, 5.5, 5.5)"

E *underarm to hem* 13.5 (13.5, 14, 14, 14, 13.5)(13.5, 13.5, 13.5, 13.5, 13.5)"

F *armhole depth* 7.5 (8, 8, 8.5, 9, 9.25)(9.75, 10.25, 10.75, 11.25, 11.75)"

G *shoulder drop* 2"

H *back length* 23 (23.5, 24, 24.5, 25, 24.75)(25.25, 25.75, 26.25, 26.75, 27.25)"

I *front neck drop* 2.25 (2.25, 2.5, 2.5, 2.5, 2.5)(2.5, 3, 3, 3, 3)"

J *wrist width* 8.75 (8.75, 9, 9.5, 9.5, 10.75)(10.75, 11.5, 11.5, 12.5, 12.5)"

K *sleeve width* 14.5 (15, 15.5, 16.5, 17.25, 19)(19.75, 21.25, 22.5, 24, 24.75)"

L *saddle width* 3 (3, 3, 3, 3, 3.75)(3.75, 3.75, 3.75, 3.75, 3.75)"

M *sleeve seam length* 17 (16.25, 16.5, 16.75, 16.75, 16.5)(16.5, 16.25, 16.25, 16.25, 16.25)"

N *sleeve cap depth* 5.75 (6.25, 6.5, 6.75, 7.75, 7.75)(8.25, 8.5, 9.25, 9.5, 10.25)"

O *saddle length* 4 (4, 4, 4, 4.25, 4.5)(4.75, 4.75, 5, 5.25, 5.25)"

P *full sleeve length* 26.75 (26.5, 27, 27.5, 28.75, 28.75)(29.5, 29.5, 30.5, 31, 31.75)"

## 18-st Diamonds Chart, for Sizes 38 (39.75, 42.75, 46.5, 50.25, -)(-, -, -, -, -)"

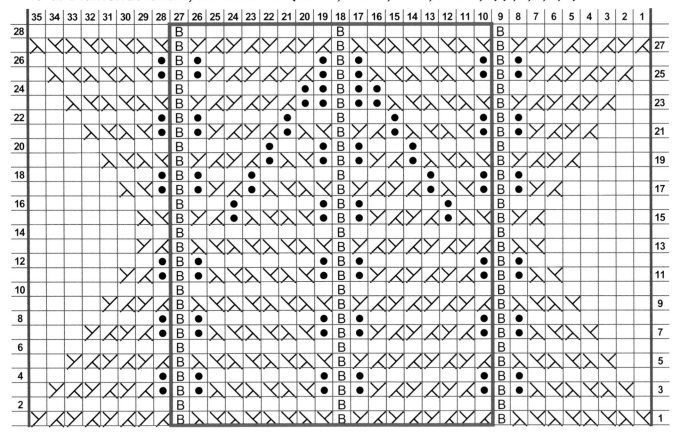

## 22-st Diamonds Chart, for Sizes - (-, -, -, -, 54.5)(57.75, 62.5, 65.75, 70.25, 73.75)"

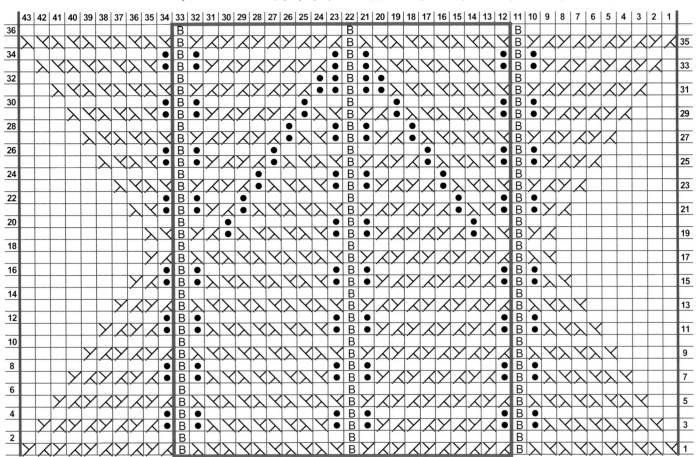

# GANNET

by Kristen TenDyke

### FINISHED MEASUREMENTS

34.75 (38.5, 43.25, 47, 50.75)(54.75, 59.25, 63, 66.75)" finished chest circumference, meant to be worn with 2-4" positive ease
*Sample is 38.5" size; model is 31" chest*

### YARN

Twill™ (worsted weight, 100% Superwash Merino Wool; 149 yards/100g): Crabapple 27933, 9 (10, 11, 12, 12)(13, 14, 15, 15) hanks

### NEEDLES

US 8 (5mm) 24-32" circular needles and set of DPNs, or size to obtain gauge
US 7 (4.5mm) 24-32" circular needles and set of DPNs, or one size smaller than size used to obtain gauge

### NOTIONS

Yarn Needle
Stitch Markers
Locking Stitch Markers
Cable Needle
Scrap Yarn or Stitch Holder
Size G/6 Crochet Hook and Scrap Yarn

### GAUGE

17 sts and 24 rows = 4" in Stockinette Stitch flat and in the round, blocked
22 sts = 5" in Left and Right Edge Cable Panels flat and in the round, blocked
24 sts = 6" in Center Cable Panel flat and in the round, blocked

For pattern support, contact kristen@kristentendyke.com

# Gannet

*Notes:*

Cables go hand in hand with cozy, and cozy is a cabled hoodie with a big kangaroo pocket. These elements of coziness are combined with our favorite top-down, seamless sweater techniques in the Gannet hoodie.

The hood is shaped from the top down to the neck, where shoulder stitches are cast on and the back pattern is established. Front shoulder stitches are picked up, then sleeve stitches are picked up from the back and front. The yoke is worked with contiguous sleeve shaping to the underarms. Body and sleeves are divided and worked separately. A seamless pocket is worked on the front during the waist shaping.

Use larger needle throughout. The smaller needle is used only for the ribbing at the end of the Body and Sleeves.

Charts are worked both in the round and flat. When working charts in the round, read each chart row from right to left as a RS row; when working charts flat, read RS rows (even numbers) from right to left, and WS rows (odd numbers) from left to right.

**LLI (Left Lifted Increase)**
Knit into the left shoulder of the stitch two rows below the stitch on the RH needle.

**LLPI (Left Lifted Purl Increase)**
Purl into the left shoulder of the stitch two rows below the stitch on the RH needle.

**RLI (Right Lifted Increase)**
Knit into the right shoulder of the stitch one row below the stitch on the LH needle.

**RLPI (Right Lifted Purl Increase)**
Purl into the right shoulder of the stitch one row below the stitch on the LH needle.

**LT (Left Twist)**
Sl1 st to CN and hold in front; K1; K1 from CN.

**LPT (Left Twist, Purl back)**
Sl1 st to CN and hold in front; P1; K1 from CN.

**RT (Right Twist)**
Sl1 st to CN and hold in back; K1; K1 from CN.

**RPT (Right Twist, Purl back)**
Sl1 st to CN and hold in back; K1; P1 from CN.

**2x2 Rib (in the round over a multiple of 4 sts)**
**Rnd 1:** (K1, P2, K1) to end.
Rep Rnd 1 for pattern.

**Right Edge Panel (flat over 11 sts)**
**Row 1 (WS):** P1 TBL, K1, P1, K4, P1, K3.
**Row 2 (RS):** P2, RPT, P6, K1 TBL.
**Row 3:** P1 TBL, K7, P1, K2.
**Row 4:** K1, RPT, P2, LPT, P3, K1 TBL.

**Row 5:** P1 TBL, K3, P1, K4, P1, K1.
**Row 6:** P6, LPT, P2, K1 TBL.
**Row 7:** P1 TBL, K2, P1, K7.
**Row 8:** P3, RPT, P2, LPT, P1, K1 TBL.
Rep Rows 1–8 for pattern.

**Right Edge Panel (in the round over 11 sts)**
**Rnd 1:** P3, K1, P4, K1, P1, K1 TBL.
**Rnd 2:** P2, RPT, P6, K1 TBL.
**Rnd 3:** P2, K1, P7, K1 TBL
**Rnd 4:** P1, RPT, P2, LPT, P3, K1 TBL.
**Rnd 5:** P1, K1, P4, K1, P3, K1 TBL.
**Rnd 6:** P6, LPT, P2, K1 TBL.
**Rnd 7:** P7, K1, P2, K1 TBL.
**Rnd 8:** P3, RPT, P2, LPT, P1, K1 TBL.
Rep Rnds 1–8 for pattern.

**Left Edge Panel (flat over 11 sts)**
**Row 1 (WS):** K3, P1, K4, P1, K1, P1 TBL.
**Row 2 (RS):** K1 TBL, P6, LPT, P2.
**Row 3:** K2, P1, K7, P1 TBL.
**Row 4:** K1 TBL, P3, RPT, P2, LPT, P1.
**Row 5:** K1, P1, K4, P1, K3, P1 TBL.
**Row 6:** K1 TBL, P2, RPT, P6.
**Row 7:** K7, P1, K2, P1 TBL.
**Row 8:** K1 TBL, P1, RPT, P2, LPT, P3.
Rep Rows 1–8 for pattern.

**Left Edge Panel (in the round over 11 sts)**
**Rnd 1:** K1 TBL, P1, K1, P4, K1, P3.
**Rnd 2:** K1 TBL, P6, LPT, P2.
**Rnd 3:** K1 TBL, P7, K1, P2.
**Rnd 4:** K1 TBL, P3, RPT, P2, LPT, P1.
**Rnd 5:** K1 TBL, P3, K1, P4, K1, P1.
**Rnd 6:** K1 TBL, P2, RPT, P6.
**Rnd 7:** K1 TBL, P2, K1, P7.
**Rnd 8:** K1 TBL, P1, RPT, P2, LPT, P3.
Rep Rnds 1–8 for pattern.

**Center Panel (flat over 12 sts)**
**Row 1 and all WS rows:** P across.
**Row 2 (RS):** P5, RT, P5.
**Row 4:** P4, RT, LT, P4.
**Row 6:** P4, K4, P4.
**Row 8:** P4, LPT, RPT, P4.
**Rows 10–12:** Rep Rows 2–4.
**Row 14:** P3, RT, K2, LT, P3.
**Row 16:** P2, RT, K4, LT, P2.
**Row 18:** P2, K8, P2.
**Row 20:** P2, LPT, K4, RPT, P2.
**Row 22:** P3, LPT, K2, RPT, P3.
**Row 24:** Rep Row 8.
Rep Rows 1–24 for pattern.

**Center Panel (in the round over 12 sts)**
**Rnd 1 and all odd-numbered rnds:** K all.
**Rnd 2:** P5, RT, P5.
**Rnd 4:** P4, RT, LT, P4.
**Rnd 6:** P4, K4, P4.
**Rnd 8:** P4, LPT, RPT, P4.
**Rnds 10–12:** Rep Rnds 2–4.
**Rnd 14:** P3, RT, K2, LT, P3.
**Rnd 16:** P2, RT, K4, LT, P2.
**Rnd 18:** P2, K8, P2.
**Rnd 20:** P2, LPT, K4, RPT, P2.
**Rnd 22:** P3, LPT, K2, RPT, P3.
**Rnd 24:** Rep Rnd 8.
Rep Rnds 1–24 for pattern.

## DIRECTIONS

### Hood

#### Garter Band
With scrap yarn, use Provisional Cast On method and larger DPNs to CO 6 sts. Do not join; work back and forth in rows. Knit one WS row. Place a locking M at beginning of next row to mark RS rows. Keep M in place throughout Garter Band. Knit 36 more rows, ending after a WS row. There are 18 garter ridges with RS facing.
Place 6 sts onto a st holder or scrap yarn. Do not break yarn.

#### Top of Hood
With RS facing and larger circular needle, use attached yarn to PU and K 36 sts evenly along selvage edge of Garter Band (1 st in each row worked). Cont working back and forth on these 36 sts only as follows.
**Setup Row (WS):** K1, work Left Edge Panel for 11 sts, Center Panel for 12 sts, Right Edge Panel for 11 sts, K1.
**Next Row (RS):** P1, work Right Edge Panel, Center Panel, then Left Edge Panel, P1.
Cont as established until piece measures 6 (6, 6.25, 6.25, 6.25)(6.75, 6.75, 6.75, 6.75)" from PU edge of Garter Band, ending after a WS row. Break yarn.

#### Sides of Hood Shaping
**Setup Row (RS):** Place 6 held sts onto tip of circular needle attached to right of top of hood. With RS facing, use tip of circular needle attached to left of top of hood to P6 held sts, PU and K 24 (24, 26, 26, 26)(28, 28, 28, 28) sts evenly along right edge of top of hood to other needle tip, K1, PM, work Right Edge Panel for 11 sts, Center Panel for 12 sts, Left Edge Panel for 11 sts, as established, PM, K1, PU and K 24 (24, 26, 26, 26)(28, 28, 28, 28) sts evenly along left edge of top of hood to provisional CO sts; carefully remove scrap yarn from held provisional sts and SI 6 held sts onto an empty needle, then P to end. 96 (96, 100, 100, 100)(104, 104, 104, 104) sts.

**Short Row 1 (WS):** P6, P1 TBL, K10, P to M, SM, work as established to next M, SM, P1, W&T.
**Short Row 2 (RS):** K1, SM, work as established to next M, SM, K1, W&T. 29 (29, 31, 31, 31)(33, 33, 33, 33) sts remain unwrapped/unworked at each end of row.

**Short Row 3 (Inc Row):** P to 1 st before M, RLPI, P1, SM, work as established to next M, SM, P1, LLPI, P to wrapped st from previous WS row, P wrap tog with its st, P2, W&T. 2 sts inc.
**Short Row 4 (Inc Row):** K to 1 st before M, RLI, K1, SM, work as established to next M, SM, K1, LLI, K to wrapped st from previous RS row, K wrap tog with its st, K2, W&T. 2 sts inc.
**Short Rows 5–6:** Rep Short Rows 3–4. 104 (104, 108, 108, 108)(112, 112, 112, 112) sts; 23 (23, 25, 25, 25)(27, 27, 27, 27) sts remain unworked/unwrapped at each end of row.
**Short Row 7:** P to M, SM, work as established to next M, SM, P to wrapped st from previous WS row, P wrap tog with its st, P2, W&T.
**Short Row 8:** K to M, SM, work as established to next M, SM, K to wrapped st from previous RS row, K wrap tog with its st, K2, W&T.
Rep Short Rows 7–8 another 1 (2, 2, 2)(2, 2, 2, 2) times. 17 (17, 16, 16, 16)(18, 18, 18, 18) sts remain unworked/ unwrapped at each end of row.
**Next Row (WS):** Work as established to wrapped st from previous WS row, P wrap tog with its st, K to last 8 sts, P1 TBL, P to end.

#### Establish Front Panels
**Next Row (RS):** (Working wrap tog with its st as it appears) P6, work Left Edge Panel for 11 sts, working same row to match existing Left Edge Panel, PM, K to next M, SM, work as established to next M, SM, K to last 17 sts, PM, work Right Edge Panel for 11 sts, working same row to match existing Right Edge Panel, P6.
WE as established for one WS row.

#### Body of Hood Shaping
**Dec Row (RS):** P6, work to M as established, SM, K2tog, K to 2 sts before next M, SSK, SM, work as established to next M, SM, K2tog, K to 2 sts before next M, SSK, SM, work as established to last 6 sts, P6. 4 sts dec.
WE for five rows, ending after a WS row.
Rep the last six rows six more times. 76 (76, 80, 80, 80)(84, 84, 84, 84) sts remain.
WE for one RS row.

#### Divide for Back & Fronts
**Next Row (WS):** Work 19 (19, 20, 20, 20)(21, 21, 21, 21) sts as established, SI those sts onto a st holder or scrap yarn for right front, work to last 19 (19, 20, 20, 20)(21, 21, 21, 21) sts, SI last 19 (19, 20, 20, 20)(21, 21, 21, 21) sts onto a st holder or scrap yarn for left front. 38 (38, 40, 40, 40)(42, 42, 42, 42) sts remain on needle for back.

### Back
**Next Row (RS):** With RS facing, use Cable Cast On to CO 10 (11, 12, 14, 15)(16, 18, 19, 20) sts for left shoulder, K to end of CO sts, work next RS row across back sts as established, then turn so WS is facing and CO 10 (11, 12, 14, 15)(16, 18, 19, 20) sts for right shoulder. 58 (60, 64, 68, 70)(74, 78, 80, 82) sts.

## Back Shoulders Shaping

**Short Row 1 (WS):** P to M, SM, work as established to next M, P to last 7 (8, 8, 10, 11)(11, 13, 13, 14) sts, W&T.

**Short Row 2 (RS):** K to M, SM, work as established to next M, K to last 7 (8, 8, 10, 11)(11, 13, 13, 14) sts, W&T. 6 (7, 7, 9, 10)(10, 12, 12, 13) sts remain unworked/unwrapped at each end of row.

**Short Row 3:** Work as established to wrapped st from previous WS row, P wrap tog with its st, P2 (3, 3, 4, 4)(4, 5, 5, 6), W&T.

**Short Row 4:** Work as established to wrapped st from previous RS row, K wrap tog with its st, K2 (3, 3, 4, 4)(4, 5, 5, 6), W&T. 3 (3, 3, 4, 5)(5, 6, 6, 6) sts remain unworked/unwrapped at each end of row.

**Next Row (WS):** Work as established to wrapped st from previous WS row, P wrap tog with its st, work to end as established.

**Next Row (RS):** Work as established to wrapped st from previous RS row, K wrap tog with its st, work to end as established.

WE for nine rows, ending after a WS row. Take note of which row of Edge Panels is worked last to end fronts after same row. Place back sts onto a st holder or scrap yarn. Break yarn.

## Right Front Shoulder

Place 19 (19, 20, 20, 20)(21, 21, 21, 21) held right front hood sts onto needle, preparing to work a RS row.

**Setup Row (RS):** With RS of back facing, beginning at armhole edge of right back shoulder CO sts, PU and K 10 (11, 12, 14, 15)(16, 18, 19, 20) sts along right back shoulder, then 1 st at gap between CO sts and held sts, then work to end of held sts as established. 30 (31, 33, 35, 36)(38, 40, 41, 42) sts.

### Right Front Shoulder Shaping

**Short Row 1 (WS Dec Row):** Work 19 (19, 20, 20, 20)(21, 21, 21, 21) sts as established, SSP, P2 (2, 3, 3, 3)(4, 4, 5, 5), W&T. 1 st dec; 29 (30, 32, 34, 35)(37, 39, 40, 41) sts remain; 6 (7, 7, 9, 10)(10, 12, 12, 13) sts remain unworked/unwrapped at end of row.

**Short Row 2 (RS):** Work to end as established.

**Short Row 3:** Work as established to wrapped st from previous WS row, P wrap tog with its st, P3 (4, 4, 5, 5)(5, 6, 6, 6), W&T. 3 (3, 3, 4, 5)(5, 6, 6, 6) sts remain unworked/unwrapped at end of row.

**Short Row 4:** Work to end as established.

**Next Row:** Work as established to wrapped st from previous WS row, P wrap tog with its st, work to end as established.

WE for ten rows, ending after same WS row of Edge Panels as for back.

Place sts onto a st holder or scrap yarn. Break yarn.

## Left Front Shoulder

Place 19 (19, 20, 20, 20)(21, 21, 21, 21) held left front hood sts onto needle, preparing to work a WS row. With empty needle and WS facing, work to end as established.

**Next Row (RS):** Work to end as established, PU and K 1 st between hood sts and left back shoulder CO sts, then 10 (11, 12, 14, 15)(16, 18, 19, 20) sts along left back shoulder CO sts. 30 (31, 33, 35, 36)(38, 40, 41, 42) sts.

**Dec Row (WS):** P9 (10, 11, 13, 14)(15, 17, 18, 19), P2tog, work to end as established. 29 (30, 32, 34, 35)(37, 39, 40, 41) sts remain.

### Left Front Shoulder Shaping

**Short Row 1 (RS):** Work as established to last 7 (8, 8, 10, 11)(11, 13, 13, 14) sts, W&T. 6 (7, 7, 9, 10)(10, 12, 12, 13) sts remain unworked/unwrapped at end of row.

**Short Row 2 (WS):** Work to end as established.

**Short Row 3:** Work as established to wrapped st from previous RS row, K wrap tog with its st, K3 (4, 4, 5, 5)(5, 6, 6, 6), W&T. 3 (3, 3, 4, 5)(5, 6, 6, 6) sts remain unworked/unwrapped at end of row.

**Short Row 4:** Work to end as established.

**Next Row:** Work as established to wrapped st from previous RS row, K wrap tog with its st, work to end as established.

WE for nine rows, ending after same WS row of Edge Panels as for back. Do not break yarn.

## Yoke

Cont working back and forth in rows with yarn attached to left front as follows.

**Joining Row (RS):** Work as established to end of left front sts, PM for armhole, PU and K 14 sts evenly along selvage edge to back, PM, work as established across back sts, PM, PU and K 14 sts evenly along selvage edge to right front, PM, work as established to end of right front sts. 29 (30, 32, 34, 35)(37, 39, 40, 41) sts each front, 14 sts each sleeve, and 58 (60, 64, 68, 70)(74, 78, 80, 82) sts for back; 144 (148, 156, 164, 168)(176, 184, 188, 192) sts total.

### Top of Sleeve Cap Shaping

**Short Row 1 (WS):** Work as established to first armhole M, SM, P to 5 sts before next armhole M, W&T.

**Short Row 2 (RS):** K to 5 sts before next armhole M, W&T.

**Short Row 3:** P to wrapped st, P wrap tog with its st, P2, W&T.

**Short Row 4:** K to wrapped st, K wrap tog with its st, K2, W&T.

**Short Row 5:** P to wrapped st, P wrap tog with its st, P to M, SM, work across back sts as established to next armhole M, SM, P to 5 sts before next armhole M, W&T.

**Short Rows 6–8:** Rep Short Rows 2–4.

**Short Row 9 (WS):** P to wrapped st, P wrap tog with its st, P to M, SM, work to end of left front sts as established.

### Cap Shaping

*Notes:* All lifted incs lift the st below the st beside armhole M, as opposed to the second st away from M. When working next row, K remaining wraps tog with their sts as they are reached.

**Cap Inc Row (RS):** (Work as established to first armhole M, SM, K1, LLI, work as established to 1 st before next armhole M, RLI, K1, SM) two times, work to end as established. 4 sts inc (2 sts each sleeve).

**Next Row (WS):** WE as established.

Rep last two rows 12 (11, 10, 10, 9)(9, 8, 7, 6) more times. 29 (30, 32, 34, 35)(37, 39, 40, 41) sts each front, 40 (38, 36, 36, 34)(34, 32, 30, 28) sts each sleeve, 58 (60, 64, 68, 70)(74, 78, 80, 82) sts for back; 196 (196, 200, 208, 208)(216, 220, 220, 220) sts total.

## Cap & Armhole Shaping

**Inc Row (RS):** (Work as established to 1 st before armhole M, RLI, K1, SM, K1, LLI) four times, work to end as established. 8 sts inc (1 st each front, 2 sts each sleeve and back).

**Next Row (WS):** Work even as established.

Rep last two rows 2 (4, 6, 7, 9)(10, 12, 14, 16) more times. 32 (35, 39, 42, 45)(48, 52, 55, 58) sts each front, 46 (48, 50, 52, 54)(56, 58, 60, 62) sts each sleeve, 64 (70, 78, 84, 90)(96, 104, 110, 116) sts for back; 220 (236, 256, 272, 288)(304, 324, 340, 356) sts total.

## Divide Body & Sleeves

**Next Row (RS):** *Work to armhole M as established, remove M, turn work so WS is facing and use Cable Cast On to CO 5 (6, 7, 8, 9)(10, 11, 12, 13) sts, PM for side, CO another 5 (6, 7, 8, 9)(10, 11, 12, 13) sts, turn so RS is facing, place next 46 (48, 50, 52, 54)(56, 58, 60, 62) sleeve sts onto a st holder or scrap yarn, remove M; rep from * once more, work to end as established. 148 (164, 184, 200, 216)(232, 252, 268, 284) sts.

## Body

*Note:* Read following instructions before continuing—fronts are joined to be worked in the round, and waist shaping occurs AT THE SAME TIME. Work waist Dec Row in row or rnd accordingly.

### Join Fronts

Cont working waist shaping (below) in rows until next rep of Row 8 or 24 of Center Panel is completed. Break yarn. Join to work in the rnd as follows: Sl all left front sts to RH needle (beside right front sts) to begin rnd at M at left side body. Join yarn and cont working in the rnd. Change color of M to easily identify BOR.

**Joining Rnd:** Work across back as established to side M, SM, work right front to last 6 sts, work Row 9 or 1 of Center Panel over last 6 sts of right front and first 6 sts of left front, cont working to end of left front.

### Upper Waist Shaping

WE for nine rows/rnds, ending after a WS row.

**Dec Row (flat, RS):** (Work as established to 3 sts before side M, SSK, K1, SM, K1, K2tog) two times, work to end as established. 4 sts dec.

*or* **Dec Rnd (in the rnd):** (K1, K2tog, work as established to 3 sts before side M, SSK, K1, SM) two times. 4 sts dec.

Rep last ten rows/rnds three more times. 66 (74, 84, 92, 100)(108, 118, 126, 134) sts each back and front; 132 (148, 168, 184, 200)(216, 236, 252, 268) sts total.

WE for one rnd, ending after an odd-numbered rnd of Panels.

## Outer Pocket

**Setup Row (RS):** Work across back as established to side M, SM, work 13 (15, 18, 20, 22)(24, 27, 29, 31) front sts, drop yarn, PM for pocket, join second ball of yarn, work 40 (44, 48, 52, 56)(60, 64, 68, 72) sts as established for outer pocket, PM, turn. Work back and forth in rows along last 40 (44, 48, 52, 56)(60, 64, 68, 72) sts. Keep body sts on circular needle.

WE for three rows, ending after a WS row and maintaining first and last 3 sts in Garter Stitch throughout pocket.

### Outer Pocket Shaping

**Inc Row (RS):** K4, LLI, work as established to last 4 sts, RLI, K4. 2 sts inc.

WE for five rows, ending after a WS row.

Rep last six rows five more times. 52 (56, 60, 64, 68)(72, 76, 80, 84) sts.

(Work Inc Row, then WE for three rows) four times. 60 (64, 68, 72, 76)(80, 84, 88, 92) sts.

WE for one more RS row.

Place all sts onto a st holder or scrap yarn.

## Inner Pocket & Lower Body

**Pocket PU Rnd:** Using yarn that was dropped at beginning of pocket and circular needle, PU and K 1 st from back of each of the 40 (44, 48, 52, 56)(60, 64, 68, 72) pocket sts, work to end of rnd as established. 132 (148, 168, 184, 200)(216, 236, 252, 268) sts.

WE for seven rnds, working back sts as established, and all front sts in St st.

### Lower Waist Shaping

**Inc Rnd:** (K1, LLI, work as established to 1 st before side M, RLI, K1, SM) two times. 4 sts inc.

WE for eleven rnds.

Rep last twelve rnds three more times. 74 (82, 92, 100, 108)(116, 126, 134, 142) each back and front; 148 (164, 184, 200, 216)(232, 252, 268, 284) sts total.

WE for one rnd, ending after an even-numbered rnd of Panels.

**Pocket Joining Rnd:** Work across back sts as established to side M, SM, work 7 (9, 12, 14, 16)(18, 21, 23, 25) sts as established, place 60 (64, 68, 72, 76)(80, 84, 88, 92) held pocket sts onto an empty needle and hold it parallel to lower body sts, join pocket and body sts tog by working 1 st from each needle tog in pattern as established, work to end of rnd as established.

Change to smaller circular needles.
Knit one rnd.
Purl one rnd.
Knit one rnd.
Work 2x2 Rib for 2.5".
BO all sts in pattern.

## Sleeves (make two the same)

Return 46 (48, 50, 52, 54)(56, 58, 60, 62) held sts from one sleeve to DPNs. Beginning at center of underarm CO sts, PU and K 6 (7, 8, 9, 10)(11, 12, 13, 14) sts along half of underarm CO edge, K to end of held sts, then PU and K 6 (7, 8, 9, 10)(11, 12, 13, 14) sts along remaining underarm CO sts. PM for BOR. 58 (62, 66, 70, 74)(78, 82, 86, 90) sts.

**Dec Rnd:** K4 (5, 6, 7, 8)(9, 10, 11, 12), K2tog, K to last 6 (7, 8, 9, 10)(11, 12, 13, 14) sts, SSK, K to end. 56 (60, 64, 68, 72)(76, 80, 84, 88) sts.

### Sleeve Shaping

Knit 5 (4, 4, 3, 3)(2, 2, 2, 2) rnds.

**Dec Rnd:** K1, K2tog, K to last 3 sts, SSK, K1. 2 sts dec.

Rep last 6 (5, 5, 4, 4)(3, 3, 3, 3) rnds 1 (2, 2, 1, 7)(3, 3, 8, 13) more times. 52 (54, 58, 64, 56)(68, 72, 66, 60) sts.

\*Knit 7 (6, 6, 5, 5)(4, 4, 4, 4) rnds, then work Dec Rnd;
rep from \* 9 (10, 10, 13, 9)(15, 15, 12, 9) more times.
32 (32, 36, 36, 36)(36, 40, 40, 40) sts.
WE in St st, if necessary, until piece measures 16″ from
underarm, or 2.5″ shorter than desired length.

Change to smaller DPNs.
Purl one rnd.
Knit one rnd.
Work 2x2 Rib for 2″.
BO all sts loosely in pattern.

## Finishing
Weave in ends, wash, and block to diagram.

## Center Panel

| | 12 | 11 | 10 | 9 | 8 | 7 | 6 | 5 | 4 | 3 | 2 | 1 | |
|---|---|---|---|---|---|---|---|---|---|---|---|---|---|
| 24 | ● | ● | ● | ● | / | ⋏⋏ | | ⋋ | ● | ● | ● | ● | 24 |
| 23 | | | | | | | | | | | | | 23 |
| 22 | ● | ● | ● | / | ⋏ | | ⋋ | ⋋ | ● | ● | ● | | 22 |
| 21 | | | | | | | | | | | | | 21 |
| 20 | ● | ● | / | ⋏ | | | ⋋ | ⋋ | ● | ● | | | 20 |
| 19 | | | | | | | | | | | | | 19 |
| 18 | ● | ● | | | | | | | ● | ● | | | 18 |
| 17 | | | | | | | | | | | | | 17 |
| 16 | ● | ● | ⋌ | ⋋ | | | ⋌ | ⋋ | ● | ● | | | 16 |
| 15 | | | | | | | | | | | | | 15 |
| 14 | ● | ● | ● | ⋌ | ⋋ | | ⋌ | ⋋ | ● | ● | | | 14 |
| 13 | | | | | | | | | | | | | 13 |
| 12 | ● | ● | ● | ● | ⋌ | ⋏⋏ | ⋋ | ● | ● | ● | ● | | 12 |
| 11 | | | | | | | | | | | | | 11 |
| 10 | ● | ● | ● | ● | ⋌ | ⋋ | ● | ● | ● | ● | | | 10 |
| 9 | | | | | | | | | | | | | 9 |
| 8 | ● | ● | ● | ● | / | ⋏⋏ | | ⋋ | ● | ● | ● | | 8 |
| 7 | | | | | | | | | | | | | 7 |
| 6 | ● | ● | ● | | | | | ● | ● | ● | ● | | 6 |
| 5 | | | | | | | | | | | | | 5 |
| 4 | ● | ● | ● | ⋌ | ⋏⋏ | ⋋ | ● | ● | ● | ● | | | 4 |
| 3 | | | | | | | | | | | | | 3 |
| 2 | ● | ● | ● | ● | ⋌ | ⋋ | ● | ● | ● | ● | | | 2 |
| 1 | | | | | | | | | | | | | 1 |

## LEGEND

**K**
RS: Knit stitch
WS: Purl stitch

**P**
RS: Purl stitch
WS: Knit stitch

**K TBL**
RS: Knit stitch through the back loop
WS: Purl stitch through the back loop

**Right Twist (RT)**
Sl1 to CN, hold in back; K1, K1 from CN

**Left Twist (LT)**
Sl1 to CN, hold in front; K1, K1 from CN

**Right Twist, Purl back (RPT)**
Sl1 to CN, hold in back; K1, P1 from CN

**Left Twist, Purl back (LPT)**
Sl1 to CN, hold in front; P1, K1 from CN

## Left Edge Panel

| | 11 | 10 | 9 | 8 | 7 | 6 | 5 | 4 | 3 | 2 | 1 | |
|---|---|---|---|---|---|---|---|---|---|---|---|---|
| 8 | ● | ● | ● | ⋌ | ⋋ | ● | ● | / | ⋏ | ● | B | 8 |
| 7 | ● | ● | ● | ● | ● | ● | | ● | ● | B | | 7 |
| 6 | ● | ● | ● | ● | ● | / | ⋏ | ● | ● | B | | 6 |
| 5 | ● | | ● | ● | ● | ● | | ● | ● | B | | 5 |
| 4 | ● | ⋌ | ⋋ | ● | ● | / | ⋏ | ● | ● | B | | 4 |
| 3 | ● | ● | | ● | ● | ● | | ● | ● | B | | 3 |
| 2 | ● | ● | ⋌ | ⋋ | ● | ● | ● | ● | ● | B | | 2 |
| 1 | ● | ● | ● | | ● | ● | ● | | ● | B | | 1 |

## Right Edge Panel

| | 11 | 10 | 9 | 8 | 7 | 6 | 5 | 4 | 3 | 2 | 1 | |
|---|---|---|---|---|---|---|---|---|---|---|---|---|
| 8 | B | ● | ⋌ | ⋋ | ● | ● | / | ⋏ | ● | ● | ● | 8 |
| 7 | B | ● | ● | | ● | ● | ● | | ● | ● | ● | 7 |
| 6 | B | ● | ⋌ | ⋋ | ● | ● | ● | ● | ● | ● | ● | 6 |
| 5 | B | ● | ● | | ● | ● | ● | | ● | ● | ● | 5 |
| 4 | B | ● | ● | ⋌ | ⋋ | ● | ● | / | ⋏ | ● | ● | 4 |
| 3 | B | ● | ● | ● | ● | ● | | ● | ● | ● | ● | 3 |
| 2 | B | ● | ● | ● | ● | ● | / | ⋏ | ● | ● | ● | 2 |
| 1 | B | ● | ● | ● | ● | ● | | ● | ● | ● | ● | 1 |

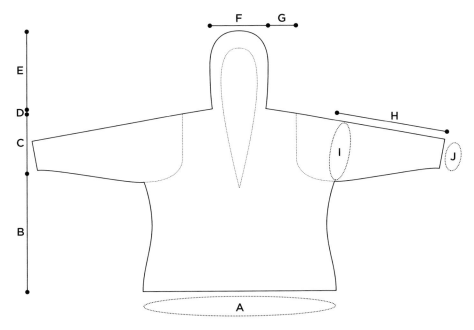

**A** *body circumference* 34.75 (38.5, 43.25, 47, 50.75)(54.5, 59.25, 63, 66.75)″
**B** *length to underarm* 19″
**C** *sleeve opening height* 7.25 (7.5, 7.75, 8.25, 8.5)(8.75, 9.25, 9.5, 9.75)″
**D** *shoulder drop* 0.75″
**E** *hood length* 12.25″
**F** *hood width* 8.5 (8.5, 9, 9, 9)(9.5, 9.5, 9.5, 9.5)″
**G** *shoulder width* 2.25 (2.5, 2.75, 3.25, 3.5)(3.75, 4.25, 4.5, 4.75)″
**H** *sleeve length from underarm* 18.5″
**I** *upper sleeve circumference* 13.25 (14, 15, 16, 17)(18, 18.75, 19.75, 20.75)″
**J** *cuff circumference* 7.5 (7.5, 8.5, 8.5, 8.5)(8.5, 9.5, 9.5, 9.5)″

# MONTE RIO

by Stephannie Tallent

### FINISHED MEASUREMENTS

33 (36.5, 40, 44.5, 49)(53.25, 57, 61.25, 65)" finished chest circumference, meant to be worn with 4–5" positive ease
*Sample is 36.5" size; model is 31" chest*

### YARN

Woodland Tweed™ (Aran/heavy worsted weight, 80% Merino Wool, 15% Baby Alpaca, 5% Viscose; 180 yards/100g): Bare 27614, 6 (6, 7, 7, 8)(9, 9, 10, 10) hanks

### NEEDLES

US 8 (5mm) circular needles, or size to obtain gauge

US 7 (4.5mm) circular needles for ribbing, or one size smaller than size used to obtain gauge

### NOTIONS

Yarn Needle
Stitch Markers
Removable Stitch Markers
Cable Needles
Scrap Yarn or Stitch Holder
Blocking Pins and/or Wires

### GAUGE

26 sts and 28 rows = 4" in Cable Pattern using Swatch Chart, blocked
18 sts and 28 rows = 4" in Broken Rib, blocked

For pattern support, contact stephannie@sunsetcat.com

# Monte Rio

*Notes:*

The tiny hamlet of Monte Rio sits next to the beautiful Russian River in Northern California. The Monte Rio pullover reflects the sandy beaches and gentle turns of the river.

The pullover is worked top down from the ribbed neck and saddle straps. After armhole shaping, the front and back are joined in the round. Sleeve stitches are picked up around the armhole and include the reserved saddle strap stitches.

Charts are worked both in the round and flat. When working charts in the round, read each chart row from right to left as a RS row; when working charts flat, read RS rows (odd numbers) from right to left, and WS rows (even numbers) from left to right.

### Cable Decrease (worked on WS row or even rnd)

Sl3 K-wise (one at a time) to RH needle. Working on RH needle, pass middle st over leftmost st (hereafter called "center st"). Sl center st back to LH needle and pass next st on LH needle over it. Sl center st back to RH needle and pass last slipped st over it. Sl center st back to LH needle and Sl next st over it. Sl center st K-wise WYIF if st would be a P st to maintain Broken Rib pattern, or WYIB if st would be a K st. 4 sts dec.

### Broken Rib (flat over an even number of sts)
**Row 1 (RS):** Knit across.
**Row 2 (WS):** (K1, P1) to end.
Rep Rows 1–2 for pattern.

### Broken Rib (flat over an odd number of sts)
**Row 1 (RS):** Knit across.
**Row 2 (WS):** (K1, P1) to last st, K1.
Rep Rows 1–2 for pattern.

### Broken Rib (in the round over an even number of sts)
**Rnd 1:** Knit.
**Rnd 2:** (K1, P1) to end.
Rep Rnds 1–2 for pattern.

### Broken Rib (in the round over an odd number of sts)
**Rnd 1:** Knit.
**Rnd 2:** (K1, P1) to last st, K1.
Rep Rnds 1–2 for pattern.

## DIRECTIONS

### Neckline
**Neckline Ribbing**
With smaller needles, CO 90 (90, 90, 96, 96)(96, 100, 100, 100) sts using your favorite stretchy CO. Join in the rnd, being careful not to twist sts. PM for BOR.
Work 1x1 Rib for 1.5".

**Neckline Incs**
**Inc Rnd:** P1, M1P, P1, K2, M1, K1, P1, M1, P1, K1, P1, M1, P1, K2, M1, K1, P1, M1P, P1, PM (for first saddle strap), K1, (M1, K1) 4 (4, 4, 3, 3)(7, 4, 14, 14) times, (M1, K2) 10 (10, 10, 12, 12)(8, 12, 2, 2)

times, (M1, K1) 4 (4, 4, 4, 4)(8, 5, 15, 15) times, M1, K1, PM (for front), P1, M1P, P1, K2, M1, K1, P1, M1, P1, K1, P1, M1, P1, K2, M1, K1, P1, M1P, P1, PM (for second saddle strap), K1, (M1, K1) 4 (4, 4, 3, 3)(7, 4, 14, 14) times, (M1, K2) 10 (10, 10, 12, 12)(8, 12, 2, 2) times, (M1, K1) 4 (4, 4, 4, 4)(8, 5, 15, 15) times, M1, K1, PM (for back).

49 (49, 49, 53, 53)(57, 57, 67, 67) sts each for front and back, 21 sts each sleeve; 140 (140, 140, 148, 148)(156, 156, 176, 176) sts total.

### Saddle Straps
Change to larger needles.
Saddle straps are worked flat, perpendicular to neckband. Work appropriately sized Sleeve chart for Saddle Strap.

**First Strap**
**Row 1 (RS):** Work Row 1 of Sleeve chart, turn.
**Row 2 (WS):** Work Row 2 of Sleeve chart to BOR M, remove M, turn.
Cont working Sleeve chart flat, ending on Row 24 (26, 28, 28, 30)(32, 32, 32, 32) (ready to begin next RS row). Break yarn. Place saddle strap sts on scrap yarn or st holder.

**Second Strap**
Sl next 49 (49, 49, 53, 53)(57, 57, 67, 67) sts to a second needle or scrap yarn to reserve for Front. Remove M. Strap is worked over next 21 sts.
**Row 1 (RS):** Join yarn. Work Row 1 of Sleeve chart to M, remove M, turn.
**Row 2 (WS):** Work Row 2 of Sleeve chart, turn.
Cont working Sleeve chart flat, ending on Row 24 (26, 28, 28, 30)(32, 32, 32, 32) (ready to begin next RS row). Break yarn. Place saddle strap sts on scrap yarn or st holder.

### Front
Use charts for the size being worked.
**Row 1 (RS):** PU and K 21 (22, 24, 24, 26)(27, 27, 27, 27) sts along edge of saddle strap just worked; work Row 1 of Size 33" Full Chart or First Rows chart for all other sizes; PU and K 21 (22, 24, 24, 26)(26, 27, 27, 27) sts along edge of second saddle strap. Turn. 91 (93, 97, 101, 105)(111, 111, 121, 121) sts.
**Row 2 (WS):** Work Row 2 of chart.

Cont in established pattern as charted, including armhole shaping, using chart instructions for size being made. For last Inc Row on Left/Right shaping charts, CO sts as charted and work them as charted; work as charted to end of that row.

Break yarn. Place sts on st holder or scrap yarn and set front aside.

### Back
Work same as Front.

After completing last shaping row with CO sts, do not break yarn.

## Body

Join front and back as follows.

Place front sts onto needles after back sts. Join in the rnd, ready to work front sts. PM for BOR.

**Next Rnd:** Work In-the-Round Chart, following instructions for size being made, across front then again across back. WE in pattern as established through end of chart.

Cont in Broken Rib pattern, as established at end of chart, until sweater measures 15 (15, 16, 16, 16)(16, 16.5, 16.5, 16.5)" from bottom of armhole, ending on Broken Rib Rnd 2. BO all sts K-wise.

## Sleeves (make two the same)

Work appropriate Sleeve chart for size, continuing from where saddle strap ended (referring to supplemental chart if needed for size being made).

**Setup Rnd:** Starting from center underarm with RS facing, PU (do not K, just PU) 19 (20, 25, 28, 30)(34, 37, 38, 39) sts (1 st in each CO st from underarm CO) along armhole edge, place 21 sts from saddle straps onto needle, PU 20 (21, 26, 29, 31)(35, 38, 39, 40) sts down armhole to underarm. PM for BOR at center underarm. 60 (62, 72, 78, 82)(90, 96, 98, 100) sts.

Work short rows to shape sleeve cap as charted. Do not conceal wraps when working wrapped sts.

**Short Row 1 (RS):** Sl18 (18, 23, 24, 25)(28, 31, 32, 33) sts, join yarn; work as charted including W&T. 23 (25, 25, 29, 31)(33, 33, 33, 33) sts worked.

**Short Row 2 (WS):** Work as charted including W&T.

Cont working short rows as charted until chart Row 40 (40, 60, 56, 56)(56, 56, 56, 56) is completed. For next row, begin short rows as follows, maintaining Broken Rib as established by first and last st column of chart.

**Next Short Row:** Work in pattern to wrapped st, W&T next st. Rep Next Short Row until 1 (2, 2, 4, 5)(6, 7, 7, 7) sts remain unworked on LH side of BOR M, 2 (3, 3, 5, 6)(7, 8, 8, 8) sts on RH side of BOR M, ending with a WS Row (working its W&T).

**Setup Rnd 1 (partial rnd):** Turn and begin working in the rnd in pattern as established to end.

**Setup Rnd 2 (full rnd):** Work in pattern as established to end. 60 (62, 72, 78, 82)(90, 96, 98, 100) sts at beginning of sleeve.

AT THE SAME TIME as working in pattern and decs, below, complete cable pattern as charted, transitioning to Broken Rib for remainder of sleeve. 10 (10, 14, 14, 14)(14, 14, 14, 14) cable sts dec.

Work in the rnd in pattern until sleeve measures 1 (1.25, 1.5, 2, 2.25)(2.5, 2.5, 2.75, 3)" from underarm.

**Dec Rnd:** P2tog or K2tog to stay in Broken Rib pattern, work in pattern to 2 sts before end, P2tog or SSK to stay in Broken Rib pattern. 2 sts dec.

Rep Dec Rnd every 10 (10, 8, 8, 7)(6, 5, 5, 5) rnds 7 (7, 6, 9, 9)(10, 13, 15, 9) more times, then every 8 (8, 7, 6, 6)(4, 4, 4, 4) rnd 3 (3, 6, 4, 5)(8, 7, 6, 13) times. 28 (30, 32, 36, 38)(38, 40, 40, 40) sts.

WE if necessary until sleeve measures approx 15.75 (15.75, 15.75, 16.75, 16.75)(16.75, 16.75, 17.75, 17.75)" from underarm or 2.25" shorter than desired length.

## Cuff

Change to smaller needles.

Work 1x1 Rib for 2.25", maintaining K columns as established by Broken Rib.

BO in pattern.

## Finishing

Weave in ends, wash, and block.

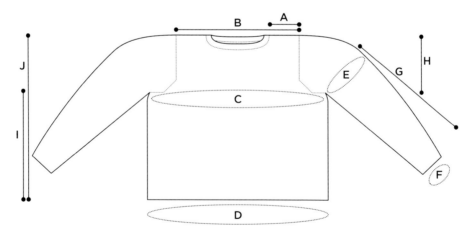

A  *shoulder width* 3.5 (3.75, 4, 4, 4.25)(4.5, 4.5, 4.5, 4.5)"
B  *crossback width* 15.25 (15.5, 16.25, 16.75, 17.5)(18.5, 18.5, 20.25, 20.25)"
C  *upper body circumference* 32.75 (36, 39.5, 44, 48.5)(52.75, 56.25, 59.75, 64.25)"
D  *circumference after transition to broken rib* 33 (36.5, 40, 44.5, 49)(53.25, 57, 61.25, 65)"
E  *upper arm circumference* 11 (11.5, 12.5, 14.25, 15)(16.75, 18.25, 18.5, 19)"
F  *approx wrist circumference* 6.25 (6.5, 7, 8, 8.5)(8.5, 8.75, 8.75, 8.75)"
G  *arm length from underarm* 18 (18, 18, 19, 19)(19, 19, 20, 20)"
H  *armhole depth* 6.5 (6.75, 7.25, 7.5, 7.75)(8.25, 8.5, 9, 9)"
I  *length hem to armhole* 15 (15, 16, 16, 16)(16, 16.5, 16.5, 16.5)"
J  *total length* 21.5 (21.75, 23.25, 25, 23.75)(24.25, 25, 25.5, 25.5)"

# LEGEND

**No Stitch**
Placeholder—no stitch made

**K**
RS: Knit stitch
WS: Purl stitch

**P**
RS: Purl stitch
WS: Knit stitch

**K TBL**
RS: Knit stitch through the back loop
WS: Purl stitch through the back loop

**P TBL**
RS: Purl stitch through the back loop
WS: Knit stitch through the back loop

**K2tog**
RS: Knit 2 stitches together as one stitch
WS: Purl 2 stitches together as one stitch

**SSK**
RS: Slip, slip, knit slipped stitches together
WS: Slip, slip, purl slipped stitches together

**P2tog**
RS: Purl 2 stitches together as one stitch
WS: Knit 2 stitches together as one stitch

**M1**
RS: Make 1 knit stitch
WS: Make 1 purl stitch

**M1P**
RS: Make 1 purl stitch
WS: Make 1 knit stitch

**CO**
Cast on 1 stitch

**W&T**
Wrap and turn for short row

**Picked Up Stitch**

**Stitch Pattern Repeat**

**Pattern Rows Repeat**

**Cable 2 Over 1 Right (2/1 RC)**
Sl1 to CN, hold in back; K2, K1 from CN

**Cable 2 Over 1 Left (2/1 LC)**
Sl2 to CN, hold in front; K1, K2 from CN

**Cable 2 Over 1 Right, Purl back (2/1 RPC)**
RS: Sl1 to CN, hold in back; K2, P1 from CN
**WS: 1/2 RPC** (Sl1 2 to CN, hold in back; K1, P2 from CN)

**Cable 2 Over 1 Left, Purl back (2/1 LPC)**
RS: Sl2 to CN, hold in front; P1, K2 from CN
**WS: 1/2 LPC** (Sl1 to CN, hold in front; P2, K1 from CN)

**Cable 2 Over 2 Right (2/2 RC)**
Sl2 to CN, hold in back; K2, K2 from CN

**Cable 2 Over 2 Left (2/2 LC)**
RS: Sl2 to CN, hold in front; K2, K2 from CN
**WS: 2/2 LC-Purl** (Sl2 to CN, hold in front; P2, P2 from CN)

**Cable 2 Over 2 Right, over center st (2/1/2 RC)**
Sl2 to CN, hold in back; Sl1 to second CN, hold in back; K2, K1 from second CN, K2 from first CN

**Cable 2 Over 2 Left, over center st (2/1/2 LC)**
Sl2 to CN, hold in front; Sl1 to second CN, hold in back; K2, K1 from second CN, K2 from first CN

**Cable 2 Over 2 Right, Purl 1 center back (2/1/2 RPC)**
Sl2 to CN, hold in back; Sl1 to second CN, hold in back; K2, P1 from second CN, K2 from first CN

**Cable Decrease**
Sl3 K-wise (one at a time) to RH needle. Working on RH needle, pass middle st over leftmost st (hereafter called "center st"). Sl center st back to LH needle and pass next st on LH needle over it. Sl center st back to RH needle and pass last slipped st over it. Sl center st back to LH needle and Sl next st over it. Sl center st K-wise WYIF if st would be a P st to maintain Broken Rib pattern, or WYIB if st would be a K st. 4 sts dec.

## Swatch Chart

## Sleeve for Sizes 33 (36.5, -, -, -)(-, -, -, -)" (See supplemental chart for size 33")

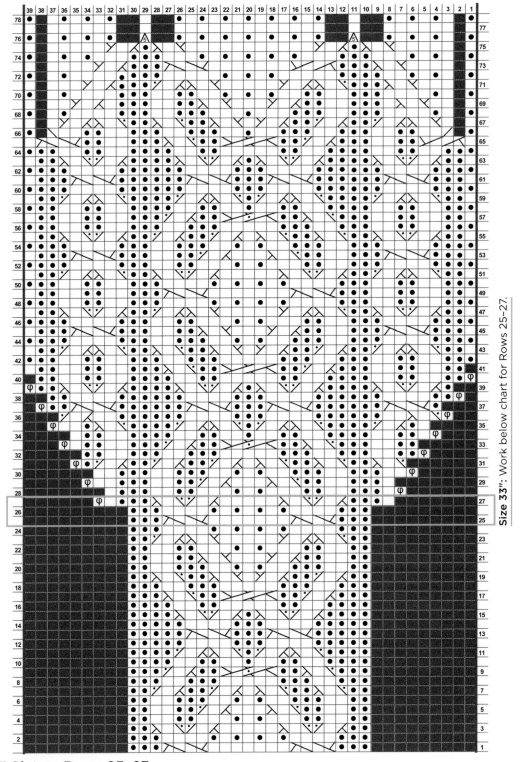

Size 33": Work below chart for Rows 25–27.

## Size 33" Sleeve Rows 25–27

## Size 44.5" Sleeve Rows 29–36 (supplemental for chart on next page)

## Sleeve for Sizes - (-, 40, 44.5, 49)(53.25, 57, 61.25, 65)" (See supplemental charts for sizes 40", 44.5" & 49")

Size 40": Work chart on previous page for Rows 29–62.

Size 49": Work below chart for Rows 31–33.

Size 44.5": Work chart on previous page for Rows 29–36.

## Size 49" Sleeve Rows 31–33

Size 40" Sleeve Rows 29–62 (supplemental for chart on previous page)

Size 33" Full Chart

After completing Size 33" Full Chart, move on to Back/Body sections, proceeding to In-the-Round Chart (omitting the center rep on that chart).

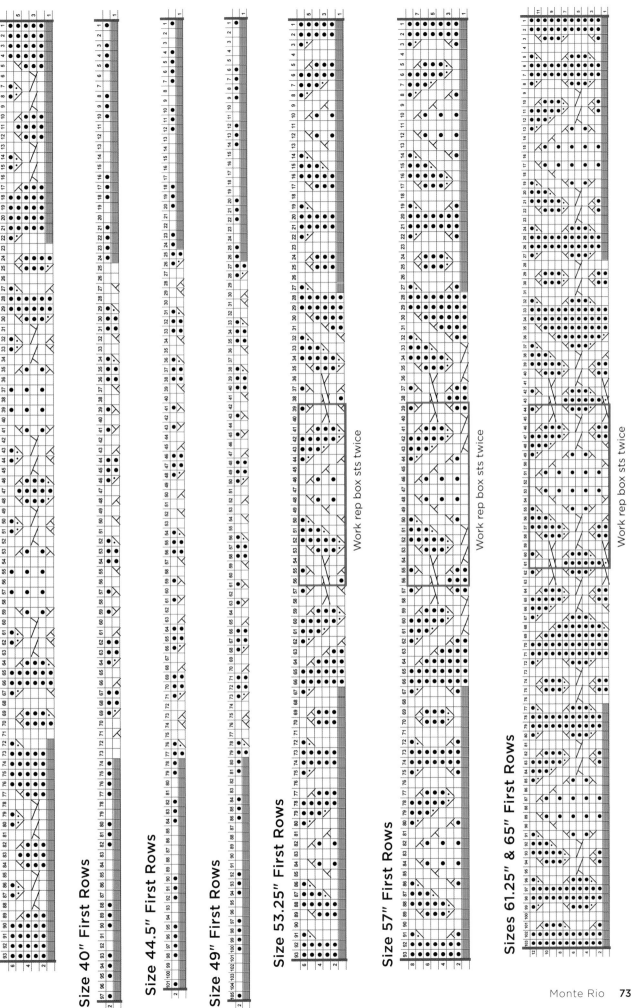

## Size 36.5" First Rows

## Size 40" First Rows

## Size 44.5" First Rows

## Size 49" First Rows

## Size 53.25" First Rows

Work rep box sts twice

## Size 57" First Rows

Work rep box sts twice

## Sizes 61.25" & 65" First Rows

Work rep box sts twice

After completing First Rows, move on to the next charts for size being worked, working chain/lattice/chain patterns as they've been established.

## Chain

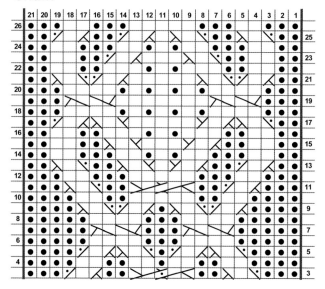

## Lattice

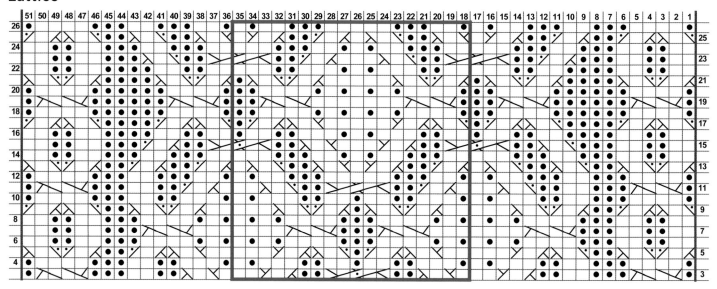

### Size 36.5" Left

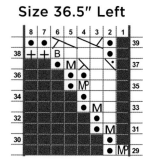

center
chart rep
Row:
19
18
17
16
15
14
13
12
11
10
9

### Size 36.5" Right

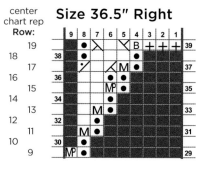

**For Size 36.5"**: Work (Chain, Lattice, Chain) beginning with **Row 11** of both charts (no extra sts on sides); work through end of charts, then work Rows 3–8. Introduce Right and Left charts on Row 9 of rep by working M1Ps after first Chain chart st and before last Chain chart st.

Work Rows 30–39 of Right chart on RH side and Left chart on LH side while working Rows 10–19 of Chain & Lattice as established between them.

## Size 40" Left

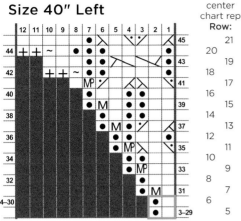

## Size 40" Right

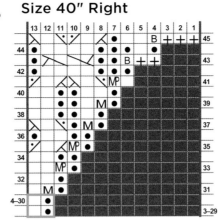

center chart rep
Row:

**For Sizes - (-, 40, 44.5, 49)**
**(-, -, -, -)"**

Between Right and Left sts, work (Chain, Lattice, Chain) beginning at bottom (Row 3). Work green boxed sts at ends of each row through tops of center charts, then rep center charts from Row 3 and begin incs on sides as charted.

## Size 44.5" Left

center chart rep
Row:

## Size 44.5" Right

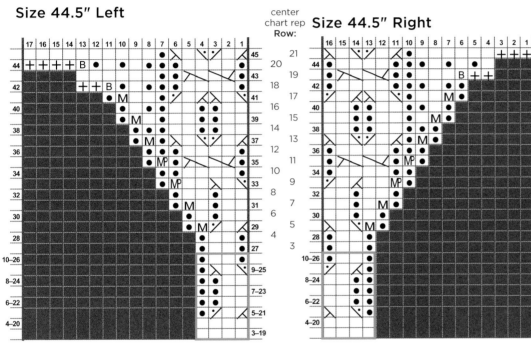

## Size 49" Left

center chart rep
Row:

## Size 49" Right

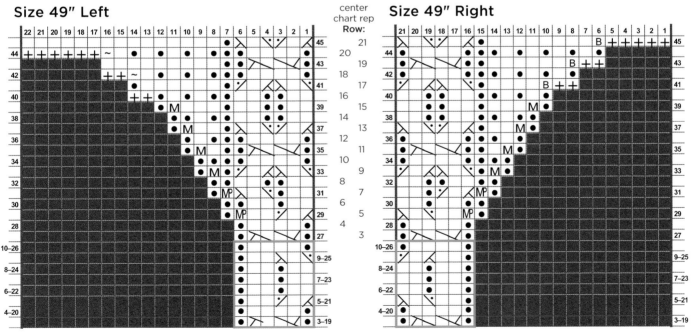

## Size 53.25" Left

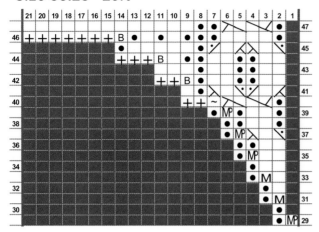

**center charts**

## Size 53.25" Right

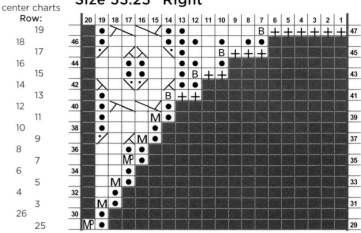

**For Sizes - (-, -, -, -)(53.25, 57, -, -)"**

Work (Chain, Lattice with red box rep sts worked twice across, Chain) beginning at bottom (Row 3) of both charts (no extra sts on sides); work through Row 24 of charts. Introduce Right and Left charts on Row 25 of center charts by working M1Ps after first Chain chart st and before last Chain chart st.

**Size 53.25":** Work Rows 30–47 of Right chart on RH side and Left chart on LH side while working Row 26 then Rows 3–19 of Chain & Lattice as established between them.

**Size 57":** Work Rows 32–51 of Right chart on RH side and Left chart on LH side while working Row 26 then Rows 3–21 of Chain & Lattice as established between them.

## Size 57" Left

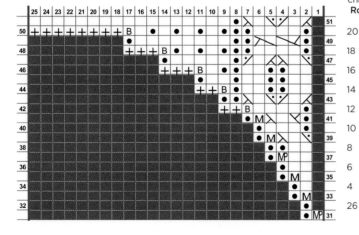

**center charts**

## Size 57" Right

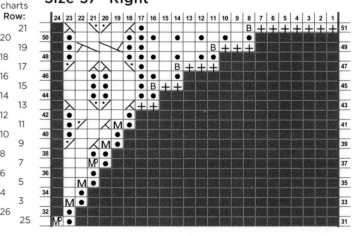

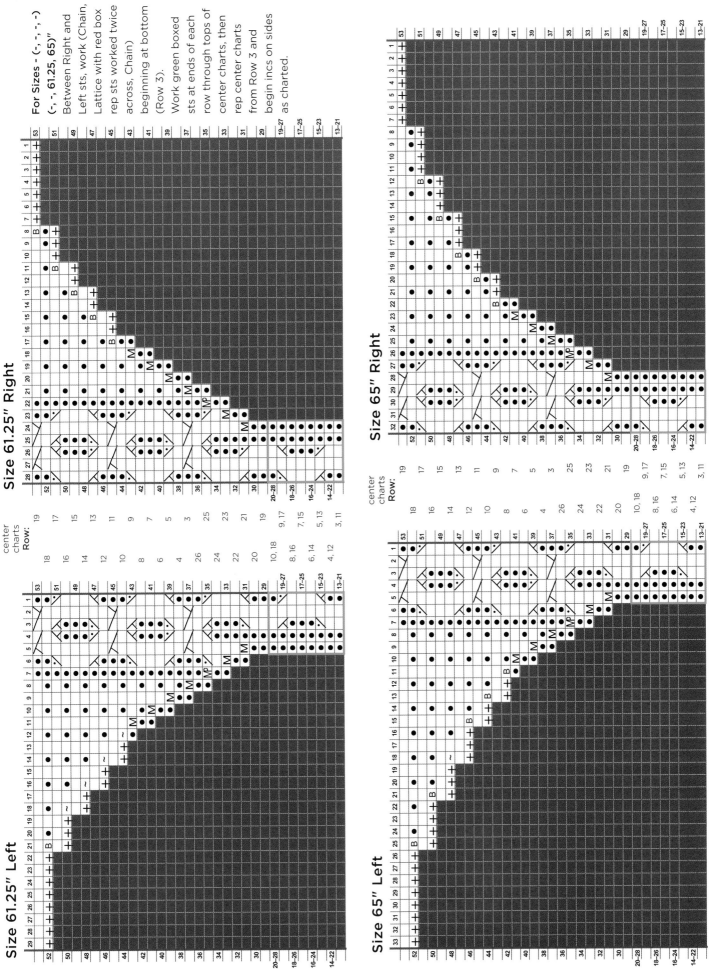

## Size 61.25" Left

## Size 61.25" Right

## Size 65" Left

## Size 65" Right

**For Sizes - (-, -, -, -)**
**(-, -, 61.25, 65)"**

Between Right and
Left sts, work (Chain,
Lattice with red box
rep sts worked twice
across, Chain)
beginning at bottom
(Row 3).

Work green boxed
sts at ends of each
row through tops of
center charts, then
rep center charts
from Row 3 and
begin incs on sides
as charted.

center charts Row:

**In-the-Round Chart — Begin with Rnd 3 (1, 3, 3, 3)(1, 3, 1, 1)**

Work blue rep box sts 2 (-, 3, -, 7)(6, 8, -, -) times.

For size 36.5", skip column 1 st and work no reps.

For sizes 44.5", 61.25" & 65", work column 1 st and work column 2 st once to start, then rep boxed sts - (-, -, 4, -)(-, -, 10, 12) times.

Work red rep box sts 0 (1, 1, 1)(2, 2, 2, 2)" times.

Work blue rep box sts 1 (0, 2, 5, 7)(6, 8, 11, 13) times; rep first boxed st 1 (0, 1, 0, 1)(1, 1, 0, 0) more time.

# MOSQUITO CREEK

by Moira Engel

## FINISHED MEASUREMENTS

35 (39.5, 44, 48.5)(53, 58, 62.5, 67)"
finished chest circumference, meant
to be worn with 4–6" positive ease
*Sample is 39.5" size; model is 31" chest*

## YARN

Twill™ (worsted weight, 100% Superwash
Merino Wool; 149 yards/100g):
Fiddlehead 27935, 10 (12, 13, 15)(17,
20, 21, 23) hanks

## NEEDLES

US 6 (4mm) straight or circular
needles, or size to obtain gauge

US 4 (3.5mm) straight or circular
needles, or two sizes smaller than
size used to obtain gauge

## NOTIONS

Yarn Needle
Stitch Markers
Cable Needle
Scrap Yarn or Stitch Holders
Six Buttons, 0.75" in diameter
Blocking Pins and/or Wires

## GAUGE

22 sts and 30 rows = 4" in Stockinette
Stitch, blocked
25 sts and 30 rows = 4" in Chart C cable
pattern, blocked

For pattern support, contact bengel@telus.net

# Mosquito Creek

*Notes:*

Mosquito Creek may not sound like an ideal place, but it is a beautiful hiking trail in North Vancouver which inspires this perfect into-the-woods cardigan. The shawl collar keeps the chilly wind at bay, and a cardigan is always the perfect choice for layering. The squirrels will be totally impressed with your amazing sense of style.

This cardigan is worked from the bottom up. Short row shoulders joined with a 3-Needle Bind Off make a polished shoulder line. Sleeves are picked up and worked from the shoulder down for a tidy set-in sleeve. The remainder of the sweater is of standard construction and features a short row shawl collar.

Charts are worked flat; read RS rows (odd numbers) from right to left, and WS rows (even numbers) from left to right. Sts to the right and left of the charts are worked in St st.

## DIRECTIONS

### Back

With smaller needles, CO 106 (118, 130, 142)(154, 166, 178, 190) sts.
**Row 1 (RS):** (K2, P2) to last 2 sts, K2.
**Row 2 (WS):** (P2, K2) to last 2 sts, P2.
Rep Rows 1–2 until ribbing measures 2.5".
Inc 2 sts across final WS row. 108 (120, 132, 144)(156, 168, 180, 192) sts.

Change to larger needles.
**Setup Row (RS):** K7 (13, 19, 25)(31, 37, 43, 49), P2, work Chart A, Chart B, Chart C, Chart D, Chart A, P2, K7 (13, 19, 25)(31, 37, 43, 49).
Work as established until piece measures 17 (17.5, 19, 19.5)(19.5, 20.5, 20.5, 20.5)".

### Armhole Shaping

BO 4 (6, 8, 9)(11, 12, 14, 15) sts at beginning of next two rows. 100 (108, 116, 126)(134, 144, 152, 162) sts.
Dec 1 st each side every other row 3 (6, 7, 9)(10, 12, 13, 15) times. 94 (96, 102, 108)(114, 120, 126, 132) sts.

WE as established until piece measures 25.5 (27, 28.5, 30)(31, 32.5, 33, 33.5)" from CO, ending with a WS row.
Using German Short Rows (see Glossary), shape shoulders at shoulder edge, as follows.
**Short Rows 1–2:** Work to last 7 (7, 8, 8)(10, 10, 10, 11) sts, turn, make double stitch (DS).
**Short Rows 3–4:** Work to last 14 (14, 15, 16)(19, 19, 19, 21) sts, turn, make DS.
**Short Rows 5–6:** Work to end of all sts, including double sts. Place 46 (48, 52, 54)(58, 64, 70, 70) center back neck sts on st holder or scrap yarn. Place both sets of shoulder sts on separate holders. 24 (24, 25, 27)(28, 28, 28, 31) shoulder sts.

### Right Front

With smaller needles, CO 54 (58, 66, 74)(78, 86, 90, 94) sts.
**Row 1 (RS):** (K2, P2) to last 2 sts, K2.
**Row 2 (WS):** (P2, K2) to last 2 sts, P2.
Rep Rows 1–2 until ribbing measures 2.5".

Change to larger needles.
**Setup Row (RS):** K17 (15, 17, 19)(17, 19, 17, 15), work Chart B, P2, work Chart A, P2, K7 (13, 19, 25)(31, 37, 43, 49).
WE as established until piece measures 17 (17.5, 19, 19.5)(19.5, 20.5, 20.5, 20.5)".

Begin armhole shaping and AT THE SAME TIME, when piece measures 17.75 (18.25, 19.75, 20.25)(21, 21.5, 21.5, 21.5)", begin Neck Shaping.

### Armhole Shaping

**Row 1 (WS):** BO 4 (6, 8, 9)(11, 12, 14, 15) sts at beginning of next row.
Dec 1 st at armhole edge every other row 3 (6, 7, 9)(10, 12, 13, 15) times.

### Neck Shaping

Dec 1 st at neck edge every other row 19 (18, 21, 23)(24, 27, 29, 26) times, then every four rows 4 (4, 5, 6)(5, 7, 6, 7) times.
Cont as established until piece measures 25.5 (27, 28.5, 30)(31, 32.5, 33, 33.5)" from CO edge. 24 (24, 25, 27)(28, 28, 28, 31) shoulder sts.

### Shoulder Shaping

Using German Short Rows, shape shoulder at shoulder edge.
**Short Row 1 (RS):** Work to last 7 (7, 8, 8)(10, 10, 10, 11) sts, turn, make DS.
**Short Row 2 and all WS Rows:** Work to end of row.
**Short Row 3:** Work to last 14 (14, 15, 16)(19, 19, 19, 21) sts, turn, make DS.
**Short Row 5:** Work across all sts, including double sts.
Place shoulder sts on st holder or scrap yarn.

### Left Front

With smaller needles, CO 54 (58, 66, 74)(78, 86, 90, 94) sts.
**Row 1 (RS):** (K2, P2) to last 2 sts, K2.
**Row 2 (WS):** (P2, K2) to last 2 sts, P2.
Rep Rows 1–2 until ribbing measures 2.5".

Change to larger needles.
**Setup Row (RS):** K7 (13, 19, 25)(31, 37, 43, 49), P2, work Chart A, P2, work Chart D, K17 (15, 17, 19)(17, 19, 17, 15).
Work as established until piece measures 17 (17.5, 19, 19.5)(19.5, 20.5, 20.5, 20.5)".

Begin armhole shaping and AT THE SAME TIME, when piece measures 17.75 (18.25, 19.75, 20.25)(21, 21.5, 21.5, 21.5)", begin Neck Shaping.

## Armhole Shaping

**Row 1 (RS):** BO 4 (6, 8, 9)(11, 12, 14, 15) sts at beginning of next row.

Dec 1 st at armhole edge every other row 3 (6, 7, 9)(10, 12, 13, 15) times.

## Neck Shaping

Dec 1 st at neck edge every other row 19 (18, 21, 23)(24, 27, 29, 26) times, then every four rows 4 (4, 5, 6)(5, 7, 6, 7) times. Cont as established until piece measures 25.5 (27, 28.5, 30) (31, 32.5, 33, 33.5)″ from CO edge. 24 (24, 25, 27)(28, 28, 28, 31) shoulder sts.

## Shoulder Shaping

Using German Short Rows, shape shoulder at shoulder edge.

**Short Row 1 (WS):** Work to last 7 (7, 8, 8)(10, 10, 10, 11) sts, turn, make DS.

**Short Row 2 and all RS Rows:** Work to end of row.

**Short Row 3:** Work to last 14 (14, 15, 16)(19, 19, 19, 21) sts, turn, make DS.

**Short Row 5:** Work across all sts, including double sts.

Join shoulders using 3–Needle Bind Off.

## Sleeves (make two the same)

Sleeves are worked in St st.

Using larger needles, beginning at underarm, PU and K: 4 (6, 8, 9)(11, 12, 14, 15) bound off sts, 40 (42, 44, 46)(46, 48, 48, 50) sts up to shoulder, 40 (42, 44, 46)(46, 48, 48, 50) sts from shoulder down, and 4 (6, 8, 9)(11, 12, 14, 15) bound off sts. 88 (96, 104, 110)(114, 120, 124, 130) sleeve sts.

## Cap Shaping

**Short Row 1 (WS):** Turn. P66 (72, 77, 81)(86, 90, 94, 98) sts, turn, make DS.

**Short Row 2 (RS):** K44 (48, 50, 52)(58, 60, 64, 66) sts, turn, make DS.

**Short Row 3:** Work to previous DS, work the next st, turn, make DS.

Rep Short Row 3 until all sts are worked except bound off underarm sts. Work final row across all sts.

## Sleeve Shaping

Dec 1 st on each side every 4 (6, 5, 5)(5, 5, 5, 5) rows  6 (17, 20, 19)(15, 20, 8, 10) times, then every 6 (7, 6, 6)(6, 6, 6, 6) rows 14 (2, 3, 6)(10, 7, 17, 16) times. 48 (58, 58, 60)(64, 66, 74, 78) sts.

Cont as established if needed, until piece measures 15.5 (15.5, 16.5, 17.5)(18, 19, 19, 19.5)″ from underarm, or 2.5″ shorter than desired length, ending on a RS row.

**Dec Row (WS):** *K10 (7, 7, 13)(14, 31, 35, 37), K2tog; rep from * 3 (5, 5, 3)(3, 1, 1, 1) more time(s), K to end. 4 (6, 6, 4)(4, 2, 2, 2) sts dec; 44 (52, 52, 56)(60, 64, 72, 76) sts.

## Cuff

Change to smaller needles.

**Row 1 (RS):** (K2, P2) to end.

**Row 2 (WS):** (P2, K2) to end.

Rep Rows 1–2 until cuff measures 2.5″.

Loosely BO all sts.

## Finishing

Seam sides and sleeves.

## Band & Shawl Collar

With smaller long circular needles and RS facing, beginning at lower right front edge, PU and K 105 (111, 120, 120)(127, 127, 127, 128) sts to first neck dec, place neck M, PU and K 40 (42, 42, 42)(45, 45, 45, 45) sts along neck edge, place shawl M number 1 (M-1), PU and K 13 (14, 15, 20)(20, 27, 30, 33) sts along remainder of neck edge, PU and K 46 (48, 52, 54)(58, 64, 70, 70) back neck sts, PU and K 13 (14, 15, 20)(20, 27, 30, 33) sts along neck edge, place shawl M number 2 (M-2), PU and K 40 (42, 42, 42)(45, 45, 45, 45) sts along neck edge, place neck M, PU and K 105 (111, 120, 120)(127, 127, 127, 128) sts. 362 (382, 406, 418)(442, 462, 474, 482) sts. Turn.

Work 2x2 Rib with short rows, as follows.

**Short Row 1 (WS):** Work 2x2 Rib, beginning with P2, to M-1, remove M-1, work 1 st, turn, make DS, replace M-1.

**Short Row 2 (RS):** Work back to M-2, remove M-2, work 1 st, turn, make DS, replace M-2.

**Short Row 3:** Work to M-1, remove M-1, work previous DS, work 2 sts, turn, make second of those sts a DS, replace M-1.

**Short Row 4:** Work to M-2, remove M-2, work previous DS, work 2 sts, turn, make second of those sts a DS, replace M-2.

Rep Short Rows 3–4 until all sts are worked between shawl and neck Ms.

Complete WS row as established to bottom edge, ending with P2. Turn.

Work 2x2 Rib as established for two rows.

**Buttonhole Row:** Work to neck M on left front, SM, work 3 (2, 2, 2)(4, 4, 4, 5) sts, BO next 2 sts, *work 22 (24, 26, 26) (27, 27, 27, 27) sts, BO 2 sts; rep from * four more times; work 4 (3, 4, 4)(5, 5, 5, 5) sts to end.

On next row, CO 2 sts over each set of bound off sts.

Cont working all sts on needle as established until bands measure 1″ and shawl collar depth is 6.25 (6.5, 6.75, 6.75) (7, 7, 7, 7)″ total.

BO in pattern.

Weave in ends, wash, and block to diagram.

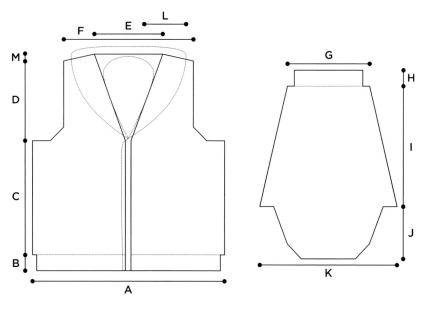

A  *width* 17.75 (20, 22.5, 24.75)(27, 29.25, 31.5, 33.75)"

B  *ribbed hem height* 2.5"

C  *side seam height, top of hem to underarm* 14.5 (15, 16.5, 17)(17, 18, 18, 18)"

D  *armhole opening* and *v-neck depth* 8.5 (9.5, 9.5, 10.5)(11.5, 12, 12.5, 13)"

E  *back neck width* 7.25 (7.75, 8.25, 8.75)(9.25, 10.25, 11.25, 11.25)"

F  *upper back width* 15.25 (15.5, 16.5, 17.75)(18.75, 19.75, 21, 22)"

G  *cuff circumference* 8 (9.5, 9.5, 10.25)(11, 11.75, 13, 13.75)"

H  *cuff ribbing length* 2.5"

I  *sleeve length, top of cuff to underarm* 15.5 (15.5, 16.5, 17.5)(18, 19, 19, 19.5)"

J  *sleeve cap height* 6 (6.5, 6.75, 7)(7.5, 8, 8.5, 8.75)"

K  *upper arm circumference* 16 (17.5, 19, 20)(20.75, 21.75, 22.5, 23.5)"

L  *shawl collar depth* 6.25 (6.5, 6.75, 6.75)(7, 7, 7, 7)"

M  *shoulder drop* 1"

## LEGEND

|  |  |
|---|---|
| ☐ | **K**<br>RS: Knit stitch<br>WS: Purl stitch |
| ⊡ | **P**<br>RS: Purl stitch<br>WS: Knit stitch |
| (chart) | **Cable 2 Over 1 Right, Purl back (2/1 RPC)**<br>Sl1 to CN, hold in back; K2, P1 from CN |
| (chart) | **Cable 2 Over 1 Left, Purl back (2/1 LPC)**<br>Sl2 to CN, hold in front; P1, K2 from CN |

|  |  |
|---|---|
| (chart) | **Cable 2 Over 2 Right (2/2 RC)**<br>Sl2 to CN, hold in back; K2, K2 from CN |
| (chart) | **Cable 2 Over 2 Left (2/2 LC)**<br>Sl2 to CN, hold in front; K2, K2 from CN |
| (chart) | **Cable 2 Over 2 Right, Purl back (2/2 RPC)**<br>Sl2 to CN, hold in back; K2, P2 from CN |
| (chart) | **Cable 2 Over 2 Left, Purl back (2/2 LPC)**<br>Sl2 to CN, hold in front; P2, K2 from CN |

### Chart A

## Chart B

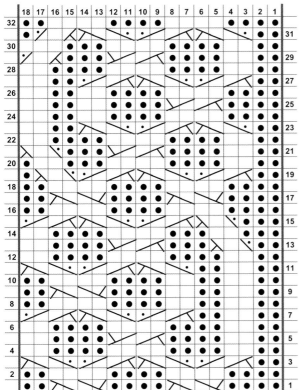

## Chart D

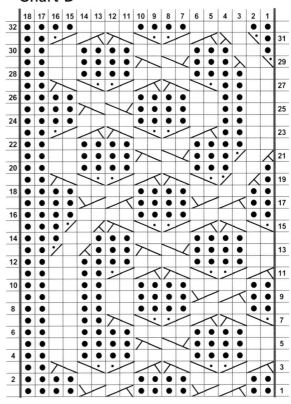

## Chart C

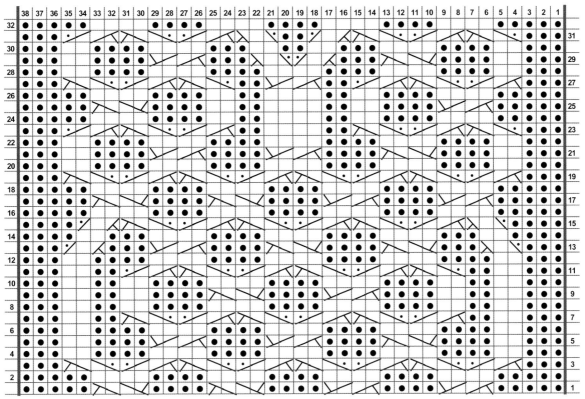

# NORTH RIDGE

by Valerie Hobbs

## FINISHED MEASUREMENTS

36.25 (40.5, 43.5, 48.5, 51.5)(55.75, 60.5, 66.25, 71)" finished chest circumference, meant to be worn with 2–4" positive ease
*Sample on woman is 40" size and model is 31" chest; sample on man is 48" size and model is 38" chest*

## YARN

Wool of the Andes™ (worsted weight, 100% Peruvian Highland Wool; 110 yards/50g): Burdock Heather 28288, 13 (14, 16, 18, 19)(21, 22, 24, 26) skeins
*or*
Wool of the Andes™ Tweed (worsted weight, 80% Peruvian Highland Wool, 20% Donegal Tweed; 110 yards/50g): Sarsaparilla 28308, 13 (14, 16, 18, 19) (21, 22, 24, 26) skeins

## NEEDLES

US 8 (5mm) 24–32" circular needle, or size to obtain gauge
US 8 (5mm) DPN or straight or circular needle for 3-Needle Bind Off

## NOTIONS

Yarn Needle
Four Stitch Markers
Four Locking Stitch Markers
Cable Needle
Four Stitch Holders or Scrap Yarn

## GAUGE

20 sts and 26 rows = 4" in Moss Stitch, blocked
62 (70, 70, 70, 70)(78, 78, 86, 86) sts = 9.75 (11, 11, 11, 11)(12.25, 12.25, 13.5, 13.5)" wide in Cable Panel, lightly blocked
13 sts = 2" wide in Right or Left Cross Cable, lightly blocked

For pattern support, contact vhobbs@rcn.com

# North Ridge

*Notes:*

This cozy pullover with its intertwining cables, shawl collar, and classic drop shoulder silhouette revisits a comfortable old favorite.

Front and back are knit separately from the bottom up with the same patterning of cables and Moss Stitch on both. Shoulders are shaped with short rows and joined with a 3-Needle Bind Off. Sleeves, with ribbed cuffs, are knit flat in Moss Stitch and sewn to the shoulders. The sides and underarms are seamed and stitches are picked up for the ribbed shawl collar, which may be overlapped in either direction when sewn in at the bottom of the neck.

Charts are worked flat; read RS rows (odd numbers) from right to left, and WS rows (even numbers) from left to right.

Garter Stitch selvage stitches are worked throughout.

**2/2 RC (Cable 2 Over 2 Right)**
Sl2 to CN, hold in back; K2, K2 from CN.

**2/2 LC (Cable 2 Over 2 Left)**
Sl2 to CN, hold in front; K2, K2 from CN.

**2/1 RPC (Cable 2 Over 1 Right, Purl back)**
Sl1 to CN, hold in back; K2, P1 from CN.

**2/1 LPC (Cable 2 Over 1 Left, Purl back)**
Sl2 to CN, hold in front; P1, K2 from CN.

**Moss Stitch (flat over an even number of sts)**
**Row 1 (RS):** (K1, P1) to end.
**Row 2 (WS):** Rep Row 1.
**Row 3:** (P1, K1) to end.
**Row 4:** Rep Row 3.
Rep Rows 1–4 for pattern.

**Left Cross Cable (flat over 13 sts)**
**Row 1 (RS):** K2, P2, K4, P2, K2, P1.
**Row 2 (WS):** K1, P2, K2, P4, K2, P1, K1.
**Row 3:** K2, P2, 2/2 LC, P2, K2, P1.
**Row 4:** Rep Row 2.
Rep Rows 1–4 for pattern.

**Right Cross Cable (flat over 13 sts)**
**Row 1 (RS):** P1, K2, P2, K4, P2, K2.
**Row 2 (WS):** K1, P1, K2, P4, K2, P2, K1.
**Row 3:** P1, K2, P2, 2/2 RC, P2, K2.
**Row 4:** Rep Row 2.
Rep Rows 1–4 for pattern.

**Cable Panel (flat over 62 (70, 70, 70, 70)(78, 78, 86, 86) sts)**
**Row 1 (RS):** P1, K2, P2, K4, P2, K2, (P4, K4) 4 (5, 5, 5, 5)(6, 6, 7, 7) times, P4, K2, P2, K4, P2, K2, P1.
**Row 2 (WS):** K1, P2, K2, P4, K2, P2, (K4, P4) 4 (5, 5, 5, 5)(6, 6, 7, 7) times, K4, P2, K2, P4, P2, K2, K1.
**Row 3:** P1, K2, P2, 2/2 RC, P2, K2, (P4, K4) 4 (5, 5, 5, 5)(6, 6, 7, 7) times, P4, K2, P2, 2/2 LC, P2, K2, P1.

**Row 4:** Rep Row 2.
**Rows 5-6:** Rep Rows 1-2.
**Row 7:** P1, K2, P2, 2/2 RC, P2, K2, (P4, 2/2 RC) 4 (5, 5, 5, 5)(6, 6, 7, 7) times, P4, K2, P2, 2/2 LC, P2, K2, P1.
**Row 8-11:** Rep Rows 4-7.
**Row 12:** Rep Row 2.
**Row 13:** P1, K2, P2, K4, P2, (2/1 LPC, P2, 2/1 RPC) 5 (6, 6, 6, 6)(7, 7, 8, 8) times, P2, K4, P2, K2, P1.
**Row 14:** K1, P2, K2, P4, K2, (K1, P2, K2, P2, K1) 5 (6, 6, 6, 6)(7, 7, 8, 8) times, K2, P4, K2, P2, K1.
**Row 15:** P1, K2, P2, 2/2 RC, P2, (P1, 2/1 LPC, 2/1 RPC, P1) 5 (6, 6, 6, 6)(7, 7, 8, 8) times, P2, 2/2 LC, P2, K2, P1.
**Row 16:** K1, P2, K2, P4, (K4, P4) 6 (7, 7, 7, 7)(8, 8, 9, 9) times, K2, P2, K1.
**Row 17:** P1, K2, P2, K4, P4, (2/2 LC, P4) 5 (6, 6, 6, 6)(7, 7, 8, 8) times, K4, P2, K2, P1.
**Row 18:** Rep Row 16.
**Row 19:** P1, K2, P2, 2/2 RC, P4, (K4, P4) 5 (6, 6, 6, 6)(7, 7, 8, 8) times, 2/2 LC, P2, K2, P1.
**Rows 20-21:** Rep Rows 16-17.
**Row 22:** Rep Row 16.
**Row 23:** P1, K2, P2, 2/2 RC, P3, 2/1 RPC, (2/1 LPC, P2, 2/1 RPC) 4 (5, 5, 5, 5)(6, 6, 7, 7) times, 2/1LPC, P3, 2/2 LC, P2, K2, P1.
**Row 24:** Rep Row 14.
**Row 25:** P1, K2, P2, K4, P2, 2/1 RPC, P1, (P1, 2/1 LPC, 2/1 RPC, P1) 4 (5, 5, 5, 5)(6, 6, 7, 7) times, P1, 2/1LPC, P2, K4, P2, K2, P1.
**Row 26:** K1, P2, K2, P4, K2, P2, (K4, P4) 4 (5, 5, 5, 5)(6, 6, 7, 7) times, K4, P2, K2, P4, K2, P2, K1.
**Row 27:** P1, K2, P2, 2/2 RC, P2, K2, (P4, 2/2 RC) 4 (5, 5, 5, 5)(6, 6, 7, 7) times, P4, K2, P2, 2/2 LC, P2, K2, P1.
**Row 28:** Rep Row 26.
**Row 29:** P1, K2, P2, K4, P2, K2, (P4, K4) 4 (5, 5, 5, 5)(6, 6, 7, 7) times, P4, K2, P2, K4, P2, K2, P1.
**Rows 30-31:** Rep Rows 26-27.
**Row 32:** Rep Row 26.
Rep Rows 13-32 for pattern.

## DIRECTIONS

### Front
CO 112 (128, 136, 144, 152)(168, 176, 192, 208) sts, using the Cable Cast On.

**Row 1 (RS):** Following either charts or written instructions, work Row 1 of Left Cross Cable over 13 sts, PM, P1, (K2, P2) 2 (3, 4, 5, 6)(7, 8, 9, 11) times, K2, P1, PM, work Row 1 of Cable Panel over next 62 (70, 70, 70, 70)(78, 78, 86, 86) sts, PM, P1, (K2, P2) 2 (3, 4, 5, 6)(7, 8, 9, 11) times, K2, P1, PM, work Row 1 of Right Cross Cable over remaining 13 sts.

**Row 2 (WS):** Work Row 2 of Right Cross Cable, SM, K1, P2, (K2, P2) to last st before M, K1, SM, work Row 2 of Cable Panel, SM, K1, P2, (K2, P2) to last st before M, K1, SM, work Row 2 of Left Cross Cable.

Cont working charts and Rib as established until 11 rows have been worked.

**Sizes - (40.5, 43.5, -, -)(55.75, -, -, 71)″ Only**
**Row 12 (WS):** Work as established, decreasing 2 sts in each Rib section between Ms as follows; SM, K1, P2, K2tog, work as established to 5 sts before M, K2tog, P2, K1, SM; rep for second Rib section. - (124, 132, -, -)(164, -, - , 204) sts.

**Sizes 36.25 (-, -, 48.5, 51.5)(-, 60.5, 66.25 -)″ Only**
**Row 12 (WS):** Work charts and Rib as established.

**Resume All Sizes**
**Row 13 (RS):** Work Left Cross Cable as established, SM, work Row 1 of Moss Stitch to M, SM, work Cable Panel Row 13, SM, work Row 1 of Moss Stitch to M, SM, work Right Cross Cable as established.
**Row 14:** Work Right Cross Cable as established, SM, work Row 2 of Moss Stitch to M, SM, work Row 14 of Cable Panel, SM, work Row 2 of Moss Stitch to M, SM, work Left Cross Cable as established.
Cont as established until all rows of charts have been worked.

Work Rows 13–32 four more times, for a total of five reps. Front measures approx 17.25″ from CO edge. Place locking st Ms at beginning and end of last row to mark sleeve placement.

**Next Row (RS):** Work in pattern as established to 12 sts past second M, place these 37 (39, 43, 49, 53)(55, 61, 65, 71) sts on st holder or scrap yarn for Left Front; BO next 38 (46, 46, 46, 46)(54, 54, 62, 62) sts, working sts as they appear (K the knits, P the purls); work remaining 37 (39, 43, 49, 53)(55, 61, 65, 71) sts as established for Right Front.

## Right Front

Cont in pattern as established until Right Front measures 6.5 (7, 8, 8.75, 9.25)(9.5, 9.5, 9.75, 10)″ from M, ending with WS row. Note the last row number worked.

Begin short rows for shoulder shaping, working in pattern as established on all rows to end of section.
**Short Row 1 (RS):** Work to last 9 (9, 10, 12, 13)(11, 12, 13, 14) sts, W&T.
**Short Row 2 (WS):** Work to end.
**Short Row 3:** Work to last 18 (19, 21, 24, 26)(22, 24, 26, 28) sts, W&T.
**Short Row 4:** Work to end.
**Short Row 5:** Work to last 27 (29, 32, 36, 39)(33, 36, 39, 42) sts, W&T.
**Short Row 6:** Work to end.

**Sizes - (-, -, -, -)(55.75, 60.5, 66.25, 71)″ Only**
**Short Row 7:** Work to last - (-, -, -, -)(44, 48, 52, 56) sts, W&T.
**Short Row 8:** Work to end.
**Short Row 9:** Work to last - (-, -, -, -)(55, 61, 65, 71) sts, W&T.
**Short Row 10:** Work to end.

**Resume All Sizes**
**Next Row (RS):** Work to end, picking up wraps.
Place sts on st holder or scrap yarn, removing Ms.
Break yarn, leaving approx 40 (42, 46, 52, 56)(58, 64, 68, 74)″ for 3-Needle Bind Off seaming.

## Left Front

With WS facing, return held sts to needle, attach new yarn at neck edge and cont in pattern as established until Left Front measures 6.5 (7, 8, 8.75, 9.25)(9.5, 9.5, 9.75, 10)″ from M, ending with RS row.

Begin short rows for shoulder shaping, working in pattern as established on all rows to end of section.
**Short Row 1 (WS):** Work to last 9 (9, 10, 12, 13)(11, 12, 13, 14) sts, W&T.
**Short Row 2 (RS):** Work to end.
**Short Row 3:** Work to last 18 (19, 21, 24, 26)(22, 24, 26, 28) sts, W&T.
**Short Row 4:** Work to end.
**Short Row 5:** Work to last 27 (29, 32, 36, 39)(33, 36, 39, 42) sts, W&T.
**Short Row 6:** Work to end.

**Sizes - (-, -, -, -)(55.75, 60.5, 66.25, 71)″ Only**
**Short Row 7:** Work to last - (-, -, -, -)(44, 48, 52, 56) sts, W&T.
**Short Row 8:** Work to end.
**Short Row 9:** Work to last - (-, -, -, -)(55, 61, 65, 71) sts, W&T.
**Short Row 10:** Work to end.

**Resume All Sizes**
**Next Row (WS):** Work to end, picking up wraps.
Place sts on st holder or scrap yarn, removing Ms.
Break yarn, leaving approx 40 (42, 46, 52, 56)(58, 64, 68, 74)″ for 3-Needle Bind Off seaming.

## Back

Work as for Front until Rows 13–32 have been worked five times. Back measures approx 17.25″ from CO edge. Place locking st Ms at beginning and end of last row to mark sleeve placement.

Cont in pattern as established until Back measures 6.5 (7, 8, 8.75, 9.25)(9.5, 9.5, 9.75, 10)″ from Ms, ending with same WS row as on Right Front.

Begin short rows for shoulder shaping, working in pattern as established on all rows to end of section.
**Short Rows 1–2:** Work to last 9 (9, 10, 12, 13)(11, 12, 13, 14) sts, W&T.
**Short Rows 3–4:** Work to last 18 (19, 21, 24, 26)(22, 24, 26, 28) sts, W&T.
**Short Rows 5–6:** Work to last 27 (29, 32, 36, 39)(33, 36, 39, 42) sts, W&T.

**Sizes - (-, -, -, -)(55.75, 60.5, 66.25, 71)″ Only**
**Short Rows 7–8:** Work to last - (-, -, -, -)(44, 48, 52, 56) sts, W&T.
**Short Rows 9–10:** Work to last - (-, -, -, -)(55, 61, 65, 71) sts, W&T.

**Resume All Sizes**
**Next Row (RS):** Work to end, picking up wraps.
**Next Row (WS):** Work 37 (39, 43, 49, 53)(55, 61, 65, 71) sts for left shoulder, BO next 38 (46, 46, 46, 46)(54, 54, 62, 62) sts for back neck, work remaining 37 (39, 43, 49, 53)(55, 61, 65, 71) sts for right shoulder, picking up wraps.

Place shoulder sts on st holders or scrap yarn, removing Ms, and break yarn.

## Sleeves (make two the same)
CO 50 (50, 54, 58, 62)(62, 62, 66, 70) sts, using the Cable Cast On.
**Row 1 (RS):** K2, (P2, K2) to end.
**Row 2 (WS):** K1, P1, K2, (P2, K2) to last 2 sts, P1, K1.
Rep Rows 1–2 until sleeve measures 2.5" from CO edge.

**Next Row (RS):** K2, work Row 1 of Moss Stitch to last 2 sts, K2.
**Next Row (WS):** K1, P1, work Row 2 of Moss Stitch to last 2 sts, P1, K1.
Cont as established for four more rows, maintaining St st edges and Garter st selvage sts.

Begin incs for sleeve shaping.
**Next Row (RS):** K2, M1L, work Moss Stitch to last 2 sts, M1R, K2. 2 sts inc.
Inc every 14 (10, 8, 6, 6)(6, 6, 6, 6) rows 2 (8, 6, 13, 11)(7, 6, 8, 8) more times, then every 12 (8, 6, 4, 4)(4, 4, 4, 4) rows 5 (1, 6, 1, 3)(9, 10, 7, 6) times, working new sts into pattern. 66 (70, 80, 88, 92)(96, 96, 98, 100) sts.

Cont as established until sleeve measures 19 (19, 18.5, 18, 17.5)(17.5, 17, 17, 16.5)" from CO edge or desired length to underarm, ending with RS row.
BO all sts in pattern.
Break yarn, leaving a length for seaming sleeve to shoulder.

## Collar
Block front and back to measurements. With RSs facing tog, join shoulders with 3–Needle Bind Off.

With RS facing, and starting at inside corner of right front neck, PU and K: 50 (52, 60, 64, 68)(72, 72, 74, 76) sts along neck edge of right front, 40 (48, 48, 48, 48)(56, 56, 64, 64) sts along neck edge of back, and 50 (52, 60, 64, 68)(72, 72, 74, 76) sts along neck edge of left front. 140 (152, 168, 176, 184)(200, 200, 212, 216) sts, or a multiple of 4.

**Row 1 (WS):** K1, P2, (K2, P2) to last st, K1.
**Row 2 (RS):** K1, (K2, P2) to last 3 sts, K3.
Rep Rows 1–2 until collar measures 6 (7.25, 7.25, 7.25, 7.25)(8.5, 8.5, 9.75, 9.75)", ending with RS row.
Work Row 1 once more.

BO loosely in pattern on RS.
Break yarn, leaving a length for seaming.

## Finishing
Block sleeves to measurements. Fold sleeves in half and mark center of BO edge. Sew sleeves to body between Ms, matching center to shoulder seam.

Lightly steam block collar if desired. Place left Garter st edge of collar (right edge for men) behind BO edge of front neck opening and keeping edges flat, sew tog. Overlap other edge of collar and seam to front neck at BO edge.

Sew side and underarm seams. Weave in ends.

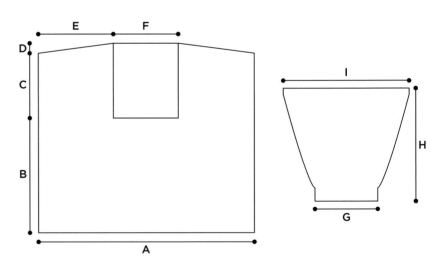

A  *width* 18.5 (20.5, 22.25, 24.5, 26.25)(28.25, 30.75, 33.5, 36)"
B  *length to underarm* 17.25"
C  *arm opening height* 6.5 (7, 8, 8.75, 9.25)(9.5, 9.5, 9.75, 10)"
D  *shoulder drop* 1 (1, 1, 1, 1)(1.5, 1.5, 1.5, 1.5)"
E  *shoulder width* 6 (6.5, 7.25, 8.5, 9.25)(9.75, 11, 11.75, 13)"
F  *back neck width* 6.25 (7.5, 7.5, 7.5, 7.5)(8.75, 8.75, 10, 10)"
G  *cuff width* 7.75 (7.75, 8.25, 9, 9.5)(9.5, 9.5, 10.25, 10.75)"
H  *sleeve length* 19 (19, 18.5, 18, 17.5)(17.5, 17, 17, 16.5)"
I  *upper arm width* 13.25 (14, 16, 17.5, 18.5)(19.25, 19.25, 19.5, 20)"

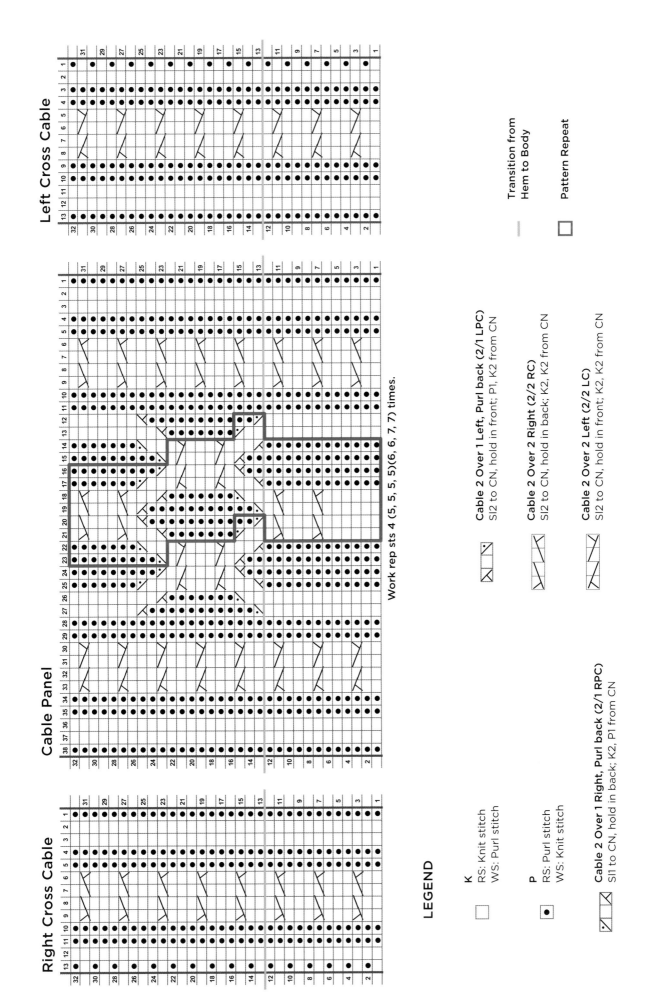

## Left Cross Cable

## Cable Panel

Work rep sts 4 (5, 5, 5)(6, 6, 7, 7) times.

## Right Cross Cable

Transition from
Hem to Body

Pattern Repeat

## LEGEND

**K**
RS: Knit stitch
WS: Purl stitch

**P**
RS: Purl stitch
WS: Knit stitch

**Cable 2 Over 1 Right, Purl back (2/1 RPC)**
Sl1 to CN, hold in back; K2, P1 from CN

**Cable 2 Over 1 Left, Purl back (2/1 LPC)**
Sl2 to CN, hold in front; P1, K2 from CN

**Cable 2 Over 2 Right (2/2 RC)**
Sl2 to CN, hold in back; K2, K2 from CN

**Cable 2 Over 2 Left (2/2 LC)**
Sl2 to CN, hold in front; K2, K2 from CN

# OSHINKOSHIN

by Mari Tobita

### FINISHED MEASUREMENTS
34.25 (38.25, 42.25, 46.25, 50.5, 52.75) (56, 60, 64, 68, 72)" finished chest circumference, meant to be worn with 4–5" positive ease for women, 5–6" positive ease for men
*Sample is 38.25" size; model is 31" chest*

### YARN
Swish™ (worsted weight, 100% Fine Superwash Merino Wool; 110 yards/50g): Copper 23882, 13 (14, 16, 18, 21, 22)(23, 25, 27, 30, 32) skeins

### NEEDLES
US 7 (4.5mm) straight or circular needles (24" or longer), or size to obtain gauge

US 6 (4mm) straight or circular needles (24" or longer), and DPNs or 16" circular needles, or one size smaller than size used to obtain gauge

### NOTIONS
Yarn Needle
Stitch Markers
Locking Stitch Markers
Cable Needle

### GAUGE
20 sts and 28 rows = 4" in Stockinette Stitch on larger needles, blocked
26.5 sts and 28 rows = 4" in Stream Cable Pattern on larger needles, blocked

For pattern support, contact maritobita@gmail.com

# Oshinkoshin

*Notes:*

The spring water from the mountains gathers to form a small stream. The small stream gathers and arrives at a cliff, twisting on the rock surface like a rope and falling down.

This sweater is worked flat in pieces. The sleeve cable runs from the top of the cuff to the neck with a saddle shoulder. The selvage stitches are included in the written instructions.

Charts are worked flat; read RS rows (odd numbers) from right to left, and WS rows (even numbers) from left to right.

**RT (Right Twist)**
Sl1 to CN, hold in back; K1, K1 from CN.

**LT (Left Twist)**
Sl1 to CN, hold in front; K1, K1 from CN.

**RPT (Right Twist, Purl back)**
Sl1 to CN, hold in back; K1, P1 from CN.

**LPT (Left Twist, Purl back)**
Sl1 to CN, hold in front; P1, K1 from CN.

**RPT-TBL (Right Twist Through Back Loop, Purl back)**
Sl1 to CN, hold in back; K1 TBL, P1 from CN.

**LPT-TBL (Left Twist Through Back Loop, Purl back)**
Sl1 to CN, hold in front; P1, K1 TBL from CN.

**RT-TBL2 (Right Twist Through Back Loops)**
Sl1 to CN, hold in back; K1 TBL, K1 TBL from CN.

**LT-TBL2 (Left Twist Through Back Loops)**
Sl1 to CN, hold in front; K1 TBL, K1 TBL from CN.

**2/1 RPC (Cable 2 Over 1 Right, Purl back)**
Sl1 to CN, hold in back; K2, P1 from CN.

**2/1 LPC (Cable 2 Over 1 Left, Purl back)**
Sl2 to CN, hold in front; P1, K2 from CN.

**LRI (Right Lifted Increase)**
K into the st one row below the first st on LH needle.

**LLI (Left Lifted Increase)**
K into the st two rows below the st just worked.

**Sloped Bind Off**
1. One row before next BO row, work to last st of row. Do not work this st. Turn work.
2. Sl first st from LH needle P-wise.
3. Pass unworked st of previous row over Sl st. The first st is bound off.
Cont to BO as usual to desired number of sts for that row.

## Stream Cable (flat over a multiple of 24 sts)
**Row 1 (RS):** K1 TBL, P2, (RPT-TBL) two times, P1, 2/1 RPC, LT, 2/1 LPC, P1, (LPT-TBL) two times, P2, K1 TBL.
**Row 2 (WS):** P1 TBL, K2, P1 TBL, K1, P1 TBL, K2, (P2, K1) two times, P2, K2, P1 TBL, K1, P1 TBL, K2, P1 TBL.
**Row 3:** LPT-TBL, (RPT-TBL) two times, P1, 2/1 RPC, P1, LT, P1, 2/1 LPC, P1, (LPT-TBL) two times, RPT.
**Row 4:** K1, P2 TBL, K1, P1 TBL, (K2, P2) three times, K2, P1 TBL, K1, P2 TBL, K1.
**Row 5:** P1, (RPT-TBL) two times, P1, 2/1 RPC, P1, RT, LT, P1, 2/1 LPC, P1, (LPT-TBL) two times, P1.
**Row 6:** (K1, P1 TBL) two times, K2, P2, K2, P4, K2, P2, K2, (P1 TBL, K1) two times.
**Row 7:** (RPT-TBL) two times, P1, 2/1 RPC, P1, RT, K2, LT, P1, 2/1 LPC, P1, (LPT-TBL) two times.
**Row 8:** P1 TBL, K1, P1 TBL, K2, P2, K2, P6, K2, P2, K2, P1 TBL, K1, P1 TBL.
**Row 9:** (LPT-TBL) two times, P1, 2/1 LPC, P1, LPT, K2, RPT, P1, 2/1 RPC, P1, (RPT-TBL) two times.
**Row 10:** Rep Row 6.
**Row 11:** P1, LT-TBL2, LPT-TBL, P1, 2/1 LPC, P1, LPT, RPT, P1, 2/1 RPC, P1, RPT-TBL, RT-TBL2, P1.
**Row 12:** Rep Row 4.
**Row 13:** RPT-TBL, (LPT-TBL) two times, P1, 2/1 LPC, P1, LT, P1, 2/1 RPC, P1, (RPT-TBL) two times, LPT-TBL.
**Row 14:** Rep Row 2.
**Row 15:** K1 TBL, P2, (LPT-TBL) two times, P1, 2/1 LPC, LT, 2/1 RPC, P1, (RPT-TBL) two times, P2, K1 TBL.
**Row 16:** P1 TBL, K3, P1 TBL, K1, P1 TBL, K2, P6, K2, P1 TBL, K1, P1 TBL, K3, P1 TBL.
Rep Rows 1–16 for pattern.

## Sleeve Cable A (flat over a multiple 16 sts)
**Setup Row 1 (RS):** P1, 2/1 LPC, P1, LPT, P2, RPT, P1, 2/1 RPC, P1.
**Setup Row 2 (WS):** K2, P2, (K2, P1) two times, K2, P2, K2.
**Setup Row 3:** P2, 2/1 LPC, P1, LPT, RPT, P1, 2/1 RPC, P2.
**Setup Row 4:** P1 TBL, (K2, P2) three times, K2, P1 TBL.
**Setup Row 5:** LPT-TBL, P1, 2/1 LPC, P1, LT, P1, 2/1 RPC, P1, RPT-TBL.
**Setup Row 6:** K1, P1 TBL, K2, (P2, K1) two times, P2, K2, P1 TBL, K1.
**Setup Row 7:** P1, LPT-TBL, P1, 2/1 LPC, LT, 2/1 RPC, P1, RPT-TBL, P1.
**Setup Row 8:** K2, P1 TBL, K2, P6, K2, P1 TBL, K2.

**Row 1 (RS):** P1, RPT-TBL, P1, 2/1 RPC, LT, 2/1 LPC, P1, LPT-TBL, P1.
**Row 2 (WS):** K1, P1 TBL, K2, (P2, K1) two times, P2, K2, P1 TBL, K1.
**Row 3:** RPT-TBL, P1, 2/1 RPC, P1, LT, P1, 2/1 LPC, P1, LPT-TBL.
**Row 4:** P1 TBL, (K2, P2) three times, K2, P1 TBL.
**Row 5:** P2, 2/1 RPC, P1, RT, LT, P1, 2/1 LPC, P2.
**Row 6:** K2, P2, K2, P4, K2, P2, K2.
**Row 7:** P1, 2/1 RPC, P1, RT, K2, LT, P1, 2/1 LPC, P1.
**Row 8:** K1, P2, K2, P6, K2, P2, K1.
**Row 9:** P1, 2/1 LPC, P1, LPT, K2, RPT, P1, 2/1 RPC, P1.

**Row 10:** Rep Row 6.

**Row 11:** P2, 2/1 LPC, P1, LPT, RPT, P1, 2/1 RPC, P2.

**Row 12:** Rep Row 4.

**Row 13:** LPT-TBL, P1, 2/1 LPC, P1, LT, P1, 2/1 RPC, P1, RPT-TBL.

**Row 14:** Rep Row 2.

**Row 15:** P1, LPT-TBL, P1, 2/1 LPC, LT, 2/1 RPC, P1, RPT-TBL, P1.

**Row 16:** K2, P1 TBL, K2, P6, K2, P1 TBL, K2.

Rep Rows 1–16 for pattern.

## Sleeve Cable B (flat over a multiple of 20 sts)

**Setup Row 1 (RS):** LPT-TBL, P1, 2/1 LPC, P1, LPT, P2, RPT, P1, 2/1 RPC, P1, RPT-TBL.

**Setup Row 2 (WS):** K1, P1 TBL, K2, P2, (K2, P1) two times, K2, P2, K2, P1 TBL, K1.

**Setup Row 3:** P1, LPT-TBL, P1, 2/1 LPC, P1, LPT, RPT, P1, 2/1 RPC, P1, RPT-TBL, P1.

**Setup Row 4:** P1 TBL, K1, P1 TBL, (K2, P2) three times, K2, P1 TBL, K1, P1 TBL.

**Setup Row 5:** (LPT-TBL) two times, P1, 2/1 LPC, P1, LT, P1, 2/1 RPC, P1, (RPT-TBL) two times.

**Setup Row 6:** (K1, P1 TBL) two times, K2, (P2, K1) two times, P2, K2, (P1 TBL, K1) two times.

**Setup Row 7:** P1, (LPT-TBL) two times, P1, 2/1 LPC, LT, 2/1 RPC, P1, (RPT-TBL) two times, P1.

**Setup Row 8:** K2, P1 TBL, K1, P1 TBL, K2, P6, K2, P1 TBL, K1, P1 TBL, K2.

**Row 1 (RS):** P1, (RPT-TBL) two times, P1, 2/1 RPC, LT, 2/1 LPC, P1, (LPT-TBL) two times, P1.

**Row 2 (WS):** (K1, P1 TBL) two times, K2, (P2, K1) two times, P2, K2, (P1 TBL, K1) two times.

**Row 3:** (RPT-TBL) two times, P1, 2/1 RPC, P1, LT, P1, 2/1 LPC, P1, (LPT-TBL) two times.

**Row 4:** P1 TBL, K1, P1 TBL, (K2, P2) three times, K2, P1 TBL, K1, P1 TBL.

**Row 5:** P1, RPT-TBL, P1, 2/1 RPC, P1, RT, LT, P1, 2/1 LPC, P1, LPT-TBL, P1.

**Row 6:** K1, P1 TBL, K2, P2, K2, P4, K2, P2, K2, P1 TBL, K1.

**Row 7:** RPT-TBL, P1, 2/1 RPC, P1, RT, K2, LT, P1, 2/1 LPC, P1, LPT-TBL.

**Row 8:** P1 TBL, K2, P2, K2, P6, K2, P2, K2, P1 TBL.

**Row 9:** LPT-TBL, P1, 2/1 LPC, P1, LPT, K2, RPT, P1, 2/1 RPC, P1, RPT-TBL.

**Row 10:** Rep Row 6.

**Row 11:** P1, LPT-TBL, P1, 2/1 LPC, P1, LPT, RPT, P1, 2/1 RPC, P1, RPT-TBL, P1.

**Row 12:** Rep Row 4.

**Row 13:** (LPT-TBL) two times, P1, 2/1 LPC, P1, LT, P1, 2/1 RPC, P1, (RPT-TBL) two times.

**Row 14:** Rep Row 2.

**Row 15:** P1, (LPT-TBL) two times, P1, 2/1 LPC, LT, 2/1 RPC, P1, (RPT-TBL) two times, P1.

**Row 16:** K2, P1 TBL, K1, P1 TBL, K2, P6, K2, P1 TBL, K1, P1 TBL, K2.

Rep Rows 1–16 for pattern.

## Sleeve Cable C (flat over a multiple of 26 sts)

**Setup Row 1 (RS):** P1, (LPT-TBL) two times, P1, 2/1 LPC, P1, LPT, P2, RPT, P1, 2/1 RPC, P1, (RPT-TBL) two times, P1.

**Setup Row 2 (WS):** K2, P1 TBL, K1, P1 TBL, K2, P2, (K2, P1) two times, K2, P2, K2, P1 TBL, K1, P1 TBL, K2.

**Setup Row 3:** P2, LT-TBL2, LPT-TBL, P1, 2/1 LPC, P1, LPT, RPT, P1, 2/1 RPC, P1, RPT-TBL, RT-TBL2, P2.

**Setup Row 4:** K2, P2 TBL, K1, P1 TBL, (K2, P2) three times, K2, P1 TBL, K1, P2 TBL, K2.

**Setup Row 5:** P1, RPT-TBL, (LPT-TBL) two times, P1, 2/1 LPC, P1, LT, P1, 2/1 RPC, P1, (RPT-TBL) two times, LPT-TBL, P1.

**Setup Row 6:** K1, P1 TBL, K2, P1 TBL, K1, P1 TBL, K2, (P2, K1) two times, P2, K2, P1 TBL, K1, P1 TBL, K2, P1 TBL, K1.

**Setup Row 7:** P1, K1 TBL, P2, (LPT-TBL) two times, P1, 2/1 LPC, LT, 2/1 RPC, P1, (RPT-TBL) two times, P2, K1 TBL, P1.

**Setup Row 8:** K1, P1 TBL, K3, P1 TBL, K1, P1 TBL, K2, P6, K2, P1 TBL, K1, P1 TBL, K3, P1 TBL, K1.

**Row 1 (RS):** P1, K1 TBL, P2, (RPT-TBL) two times, P1, 2/1 RPC, LT, 2/1 LPC, P1, (LPT-TBL) two times, P2, K1 TBL, P1.

**Row 2 (WS):** K1, P1 TBL, K2, P1 TBL, K1, P1 TBL, K2, (P2, K1) two times, P2, K2, P1 TBL, K1, P1 TBL, K2, P1 TBL, K1.

**Row 3:** P1, LPT-TBL, (RPT-TBL) two times, P1, 2/1 RPC, P1, LT, P1, 2/1 LPC, P1, (LPT-TBL) two times, RPT-TBL, P1.

**Row 4:** K2, P2 TBL, K1, P1 TBL, (K2, P2) three times, K2, P1 TBL, K1, P2 TBL, K2.

**Row 5:** P2, (RPT-TBL) two times, P1, 2/1 RPC, P1, RT, LT, P1, 2/1 LPC, P1, (LPT-TBL) two times, P2.

**Row 6:** K2, P1 TBL, K1, P1 TBL, K2, P2, K2, P4, K2, P2, K2, P1 TBL, K1, P1 TBL, K2.

**Row 7:** P1, (RPT-TBL) two times, P1, 2/1 RPC, P1, RT, K2, LT, P1, 2/1 LPC, P1, (LPT-TBL) two times, P1.

**Row 8:** (K1, P1 TBL) two times, K2, P2, K2, P6, K2, P2, K2, (P1 TBL, K1) two times.

**Row 9:** P1, (LPT-TBL) two times, P1, 2/1 LPC, P1, LPT, K2, RPT, P1, 2/1 RPC, P1, (RPT-TBL) two times, P1.

**Row 10:** Rep Row 6.

**Row 11:** P2, LT-TBL2, LPT-TBL, P1, 2/1 LPC, P1, LPT, RPT, P1, 2/1 RPC, P1, RPT-TBL, RT-TBL2, P2.

**Row 12:** Rep Row 4.

**Row 13:** P1, RPT-TBL, (LPT-TBL) two times, P1, 2/1 LPC, P1, LT, P1, 2/1 RPC, P1, (RPT-TBL) two times, LPT-TBL, P1.

**Row 14:** Rep Row 2.

**Row 15:** P1, K1 TBL, P2, (LPT-TBL) two times, P1, 2/1 LPC, LT, 2/1 RPC, P1, (RPT-TBL) two times, P2, K1 TBL, P1.

**Row 16:** K1, P1 TBL, K3, P1 TBL, K1, P1 TBL, K2, P6, K2, P1 TBL, K1, P1 TBL, K3, P1 TBL, K1.

Rep Rows 1–16 for pattern.

## DIRECTIONS

### Back

With smaller needles CO 98 (110, 126, 134, 150, 158)(166, 182, 190, 206, 218) sts.

## Hem

**Row 1 (RS):** K2, (P1, K1) 11 (14, 12, 14, 12, 14)(16, 14, 16, 14, 17) times, P1, PM, *K1, P1, K1, (P2, K2) four times, P2, K1, P1, K1, PM; rep from * 1 (1, 2, 2, 3, 3)(3, 4, 4, 5, 5) more times, P1, (K1, P1) 11 (14, 12, 14, 12, 14)(16, 14, 16, 14, 17) times, K2.

**Row 2 (WS):** P2, (K1, P1) 11 (14, 12, 14, 12, 14)(16, 14, 16, 14, 17) times, K1, SM, *P1, K1, P1, (K2, P2) four times, K2, P1, K1, P1, SM; rep from * 1 (1, 2, 2, 3, 3)(3, 4, 4, 5, 5) more times, K1, (P1, K1) 11 (14, 12, 14, 12, 14)(16, 14, 16, 14, 17) times, P2.

Rep Rows 1–2 nine more times, substituting SM for PM in Row 1.

## Body

Change to larger needles.

### Sizes 34.25 (-, -, 46.25, 50.5, -)(-, -, 64, 68, -)" Only

If working from charts, follow Setup Rows 1–8 between Ms.

**Setup Row 1 (RS/Inc):** K2, LLI, K to 1 st before M, P1, SM, *(LPT-TBL) two times, P1, 2/1 LPC, P1, LPT, P2, RPT, P1, 2/1 RPC, P1, (RPT-TBL) two times; rep from * 1 (-, -, 2, 3, -)(-, -, 4, 5, -) more times, SM, P1, K to last 2 sts, LRI, K to end. 100 (-, -, 136, 152, -)(-, -, 192, 208, -) sts.

### Sizes - (38.25, 42.25, -, -, 52.75)(56, 60, -, -, 72)" Only

**Setup Row 1 (RS):** K to 1 st before M, P1, SM, *(LPT-TBL) two times, P1, 2/1 LPC, P1, LPT, P2, RPT, P1, 2/1 RPC, P1, (RPT-TBL) two times; rep from * - (1, 2, -, -, 3)(3, 4, -, -, 5) more times, SM, P1, K to end.

### Resume All Sizes

**Setup Row 2 (WS):** P to 1 st before M, K1, SM, *(K1, P1 TBL) two times, K2, P2, (K2, P1) two times, K2, P2, K2, (P1 TBL, K1) two times; rep from * 1 (1, 2, 2, 3, 3)(3, 4, 4, 5, 5) more times, SM, K1, P to end.

**Setup Row 3:** K to 1 st before M, P1, SM, *P1, LT-TBL2, LPT-TBL, P1, 2/1 LPC, P1, LPT, RPT, P1, 2/1 RPC, P1, RPT-TBL, RT-TBL2, P1; rep from * 1 (1, 2, 2, 3, 3)(3, 4, 4, 5, 5) more times, SM, P1, K to end.

**Setup Row 4:** P to 1 st before M, K1, SM, *K1, P2 TBL, K1, P1 TBL, (K2, P2) three times, K2, P1 TBL, K1, P2 TBL, K1; rep from * 1 (1, 2, 2, 3, 3)(3, 4, 4, 5, 5) more times, SM, K1, P to end.

**Setup Row 5:** K to 1 st before M, P1, SM, *RPT-TBL, (LPT-TBL) two times, P1, 2/1 LPC, P1, LT, P1, 2/1 RPC, P1, (RPT-TBL) two times, LPT; rep from * 1 (1, 2, 2, 3, 3)(3, 4, 4, 5, 5) more times, SM, P1, K to end.

**Setup Row 6:** P to 1 st before M, K1, SM, *P1 TBL, K2, P1 TBL, K1, P1 TBL, K2, (P2, K1) two times, P2, K2, P1 TBL, K1, P1 TBL, K2, P1 TBL; rep from * 1 (1, 2, 2, 3, 3)(3, 4, 4, 5, 5) more times, SM, K1, P to end.

**Setup Row 7:** K to 1 st before M, P1, SM, *K1 TBL, P2, (LPT-TBL) two times, P1, 2/1 LPC, LT, 2/1 RPC, P1, (RPT-TBL) two times, P2, K1 TBL; rep from * 1 (1, 2, 2, 3, 3)(3, 4, 4, 5, 5) more times, SM, P1, K to end.

**Setup Row 8:** P to 1 st before M, K1, SM, *P1 TBL, K3, P1 TBL, K1, P1 TBL, K2, P6, K2, P1 TBL, K1, P1 TBL, K3, P1 TBL; rep from * 1 (1, 2, 2, 3, 3)(3, 4, 4, 5, 5) more times, SM, K1, P to end.

Begin Stream Cable pattern.

**Row 1 (RS):** K to 1 st before M, P1, SM, * work Row 1 of Stream Cable; rep from * 1 (1, 2, 2, 3, 3)(3, 4, 4, 5, 5) more times, SM, P1, K to end.

**Row 2 (WS):** P to 1 st before M, K1, SM, work Row 2 of Stream Cable; rep from * 1 (1, 2, 2, 3, 3)(3, 4, 4, 5, 5) more times, SM, K1, P to end.

Cont as established through Row 16 of Stream Cable. Rep Rows 1–16 four more times, then Rows 1–6 (6, 6, 6, 6, 6)(6, 6, 6, 14, 14) once.

Piece measures 16 (16, 16, 16, 16, 16)(16, 16, 16, 17, 17)" from CO edge.

## Armhole

BO 5 (5, 6, 8, 8, 8)(9, 9, 9, 10, 10) sts at beginning of next two rows. 90 (100, 114, 120, 136, 142)(148, 164, 174, 188, 198) sts.

Cont in pattern as established until working Row 16 of Stream Cable 8 (8, 9, 9, 9, 10)(10, 10, 10, 11, 11) times total from end of Setup Rows, then work Rows 1–8 (12, -, 6, 14, 2)(4, 8, 12, 6, 10) once more.

Piece measures 7.25 (7.75, 8.25, 9.25, 10.25, 10.75)(11.25, 11.75, 12.25, 12.5, 13.25)" from Armhole BO.

BO all sts.

## Front

Work same as for Back until 12 rows before complete, ending with WS Row.

### Left Neck Edge Shaping

Remove all Ms and place new Ms at both sides of center 14 (14, 14, 14, 16, 16)(16, 16, 16, 18, 20) sts.

**Row 1:** Work to M, BO 14 (14, 14, 14, 16, 16)(16, 16, 16, 18, 20) sts, work to end. 76 (86, 100, 106, 120, 126)(132, 148, 158, 170, 178) sts.

Use Sloped Bind Off method on following row.

**Row 2:** Work to last st, turn.

BO 6 (6, 6, 6, 6, 6)(7, 7, 7, 8, 8) sts at beginning of RS Row once, - (-, -, -, -, -)(4, 4, 5, 5, 6) sts once, 3 sts 1 (1, 2, 2, 2, 2)(1, 1, 1, 1, 1) time(s), 2 sts once, 1 st 2 (2, 1, 1, 1, 1)(1, 1, 1, 1, 1) time(s), then WE one more row, ending on WS Row.

BO 25 (30, 35, 38, 45, 48)(49, 57, 61, 66, 69) shoulder sts.

### Right Neck Edge Shaping

With WS facing, join new yarn at beginning of center BO.

BO 6 (6, 6, 6, 6, 6)(7, 7, 7, 8, 8) sts at beginning of WS Row once, - (-, -, -, -, -)(4, 4, 5, 5, 6) sts once, 3 sts 1 (1, 2, 2, 2, 2)(1, 1, 1, 1, 1) time(s), 2 sts once, 1 st 2 (2, 1, 1, 1, 1)(1, 1, 1, 1, 1) time(s), then WE two more rows, ending on WS Row.

BO remaining 25 (30, 35, 38, 45, 48)(49, 57, 61, 66, 69) shoulder sts.

## Right Sleeve

Before you start, read through this section, as incs happen at the same time as Sleeve Cable Setup Rows.

With smaller needles, CO 60 (60, 64, 64, 68, 68)(68, 68, 74, 74, 74) sts.

## Cuff

### Sizes 34.25 (38.25, 42.25, 46.25, -)(-, -, -, -, -)" Only
**Row 1 (RS):** K2, (P1, K1) 10 (10, 11, 11, -)(-, -, -, -, -) times, PM, P1, (K2, P2) three times, K2, P1, PM, (K1, P1) 10 (10, 11, 11, -)(-, -, -, -, -) times, K2.
**Row 2 (WS):** P2, (K1, P1) 10 (10, 11, 11, -)(-, -, -, -, -) times, SM, K1, (P2, K2) three times, P2, K1, SM, (P1, K1) 10 (10, 11, 11, -)(-, -, -, -, -) times, P2.
Rep Rows 1–2 seven more times.

### Sizes - (-, -, -, 50.5, 52.75)(56, 60, -, -, -)" Only
**Row 1 (RS):** K2, (P1, K1) 11 times, PM, K1, (P2, K2) four times, P2, K1, PM, (K1, P1) 11 times, K2.
**Row 2 (WS):** P2, (K1, P1) 11 times, SM, P1, (K2, P2) four times, K2, P1, SM, (P1, K1) 11 times, P2.
Rep Rows 1–2 seven more times.

### Sizes - (-, -, -, -, -)(-, -, 64, 68, 72)" Only
**Row 1 (RS):** K2, (P1, K1) 11 times, PM, (P1, K1) twice, (P2, K2) four times, P2, (K1, P1) twice, PM, (K1, P1) 11 times, K2.
**Row 2 (WS):** P2, (K1, P1) 11 times, SM, (K1, P1) twice, (K2, P2) four times, K2, (P1, K1) twice, SM, (P1, K1) 11 times, P2.
Rep Rows 1–2 seven more times.

### Sleeve Shaping (resume all sizes)
Change to larger needles.
Begin Setup Rows of Sleeve Cable A (A, A, A, B, B)(B, B, C, C, C) pattern.
**Setup Row 1 (RS):** K to M, SM, work Setup Row 1 of Sleeve Cable A (A, A, A, B, B)(B, B, C, C, C), SM, K to end.
**Setup Row 2 (WS):** P to M, SM, work Setup Row 2 of Sleeve Cable A (A, A, A, B, B)(B, B, C, C, C), SM, P to end.
Cont as established through Setup Row 8 of Sleeve Cable A (A, A, A, B, B)(B, B, C, C, C) once.

Begin Sleeve Cable pattern.
Ms establish placement for Sleeve Cable panel; remaining sts on either side are worked in St st.
**Row 1 (RS):** K to M, SM, Work Row 1 of Sleeve Cable A (A, A, A, B, B)(B, B, C, C, C), SM, K to end.
**Row 2 (WS):** P to M, SM, Work Row 2 of Sleeve Cable A (A, A, A, B, B)(B, B, C, C, C), SM, P to end.
Cont as established through Row 16 of Sleeve Cable A (A, A, A, B, B)(B, B, C, C, C); rep Rows 1–16 another 6 (6, 6, 7, 7, 8)(8, 8, 8, 8, 8) times, then work through Row 6 (10, 14, 4, 14, -)(4, 4, 4, 12, 12) once more.

AT THE SAME TIME inc at each edge as follows, starting on Setup Rows of Sleeve Cable Row 1 (1, 1, 1, 7, 7)(7, 7, 5, 5, 5).
**Inc Row (RS):** K2, LLI, work to last 2 sts, LRI, K2. 2 sts inc. 62 (62, 66, 66, 70, 70)(70, 70, 76, 76, 76) sts.
Rep Inc Row every 8 rows 11 (6, 4, -, -, -)(-, -, -, -, -) times, every 6 rows 3 (10, 13, 9, 4, -)(-, -, -, -, -) times, then every 4 rows - (-, -, 13, 23, 30)(31, 26, 25, 24, 22) times, then every 2 rows - (-, -, -, -, -)(-, 9, 12, 16, 20) times.
WE for 19 (21, 23, 27, 27, 25)(25, 27, 27, 31, 31) rows. 90 (94, 100, 110, 124, 130)(132, 140, 150, 156, 160) sts.

Piece measures 20 (20.5, 21, 22, 23.5, 23.75)(24.25, 24.25, 24.25, 25.5, 25.5)" from CO edge.

## Saddle
**Row 1 (RS):** BO 35 (37, 40, 45, 50, 53)(54, 58, 60, 63, 65) sts, M1R, pass second st over new st, K1, remove M, work Sleeve Cable panel as established, K1, M1L, SM, K to end.
**Row 2 (WS):** BO 36 (38, 41, 46, 51, 54)(55, 59, 61, 64, 66) sts, P1, remove M, work Sleeve Cable panel, P2. 20 (20, 20, 20, 24, 24)(24, 24, 30, 30, 30) sts.
**Row 3:** K2, work Sleeve Cable panel, K2.
**Row 4:** P2, work Sleeve Cable panel, P2.
Cont working as established for 30 (36, 40, 44, 50, 56)(56, 64, 70, 72, 78) more rows.
Piece measures 4.75 (5.75, 6.25, 6.75, 7.75, 8.5)(8.5, 9.75, 10.5, 11, 11.75) " including the four rows above.

### Extension (using Sloped Bind Off method)
**Row 1 (RS):** BO 10 (10, 10, 10, 12, 12)(12, 12, 15, 15, 15) sts, work to end.
**Row 2 (WS):** Work to end.
BO 4 (4, 4, 4, 5, 5)(5, 5, 5, 5, 5) sts at beginning of RS Row once, BO 3 sts - (-, -, -, -, -)(-, -, 1, 1, 1) time, BO 2 sts once, BO 1 st 2 (2, 2, 2, 3, 3)(3, 3, 3, 3, 3) times, then BO 2 sts.

## Left Sleeve
Work as for Right Sleeve until Extension.

### Extension (using Sloped Bind Off method)
**Row 1 (RS):** Work to end.
**Row 2 (WS):** BO 10 (10, 10, 10, 12, 12)(12, 12, 15, 15, 15) sts, work to end.
BO 4 (4, 4, 4, 5, 5)(5, 5, 5, 5, 5) sts at beginning of WS Row once, BO 3 sts - (-, -, -, -, -)(-, -, 1, 1, 1) time, BO 2 sts once, BO 1 st 2 (2, 2, 2, 3, 3)(3, 3, 3, 3, 3) times, then BO 2 sts.

## Finishing
Block all pieces to measurements.
Sew saddles along shoulder BO edges of front and back.
Place each end of top of sleeves at armhole on front and back and sew sleeves to body.
Sew sides of body and sleeve seams.

### Neckband
With smaller DPNs or 16" circular needle and RS facing, beginning at RH corner of back neck, PU and K: 18 (18, 20, 20, 20, 20)(24, 24, 22, 26, 28) sts along back neck, 17 (17, 17, 17, 21, 21)(21, 21, 27, 27, 28) sts along left saddle, 40 (40, 44, 44, 46, 46)(48, 48, 50, 54, 56) sts along front neck, 17 (17, 17, 17, 21, 21)(21, 21, 27, 27, 28) sts along right saddle. 92 (92, 98, 98, 108, 108)(114, 114, 126, 134, 140) sts.
Join to work in the rnd and PM for BOR.
**Rnd 1:** (K1, P1) to end of rnd.
Work 1x1 Rib for eight more rnds.
BO all sts in pattern.
Weave in all ends.

## LEGEND

**K**
RS: Knit stitch
WS: Purl stitch

**P**
RS: Purl stitch
WS: Knit stitch

**K TBL**
RS: Knit stitch through the back loop
WS: Purl stitch through the back loop

**Right Twist (RT)**
Sl1 to CN, hold in back; K1, K1 from CN

**Left Twist (LT)**
Sl1 to CN, hold in front; K1, K1 from CN

**Right Twist, Purl back (RPT)**
Sl1 to CN, hold in back; K1, P1 from CN

**Left Twist, Purl back (LPT)**
Sl1 to CN, hold in front; P1, K1 from CN

**Right Twist, TBL, Purl back (RPT-TBL)**
Sl1 to CN, hold in back; K1 through
back loop, P1 from CN

**Left Twist, TBL, Purl back (LPT-TBL)**
Sl1 to CN, hold in front; P1, K1
through back loop from CN

**Right Twist, TBL both sts (RT-TBL2)**
Sl1 to CN, hold in back; K1 through back loop,
K1 through back loop from CN

**Left Twist, TBL both sts (LT-TBL2)**
Sl1 to CN, hold in front; K1 through back loop,
K1 through back loop from CN

**Cable 2 Over 1 Right, Purl back (2/1 RPC)**
Sl1 to CN, hold in back; K2, P1 from CN

**Cable 2 Over 1 Left, Purl back (2/1 LPC)**
Sl2 to CN, hold in front; P1, K2 from CN

— **Above Line is Repeat Rows**

## Stream Cable

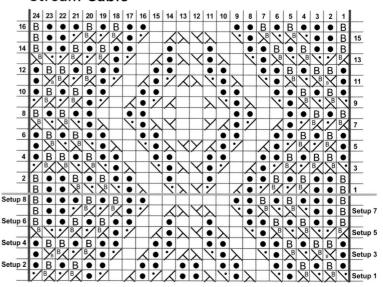

## Sleeve Cable A

## Sleeve Cable B

## Sleeve Cable C

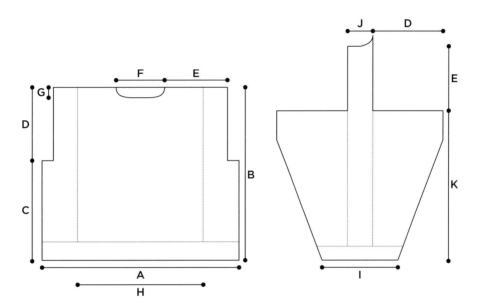

A  *chest width* 17.5 (19.5, 21.5, 23.5, 25.75, 26.75)(28.5, 30.5, 32.5, 34.5, 36.5)"

B  *body length* 23.25 (23.75, 24.25, 25.25, 26.25, 26.75)(27.25, 27.75, 28.25, 29.5, 30.25)"

C  *side seam length* 16 (16, 16, 16, 16, 16)(16, 16, 16, 17, 17)"

D  *armhole depth* 7.25 (7.75, 8.25, 9.25, 10.25, 10.75)(11.25, 11.75, 12.25, 12.5, 13.25)"

E  *shoulder width* 4.75 (5.75, 6.25, 6.75, 7.75, 8.5)(8.5, 9.75, 10.5, 11, 11.75)"

F  *neck width* 6 (6, 6.75, 6.75, 7, 7)(7.5, 7.5, 7.75, 8.5, 9)"

G  *neck depth* 1.75"

H  *cable panel width* 7.5 (7.5, 11, 11, 14.75, 14.75)(14.75, 18.5, 18.5, 22, 22)"

I  *cuff width* 11.25 (11.25, 12, 12, 12.5, 12.5)(12.5, 12.5, 13.5, 13.5, 13.5)"

J  *saddle width* 3 (3, 3, 3, 3.5, 3.5)(3.5, 3.5, 4.5, 4.5, 4.5)"

K  *sleeve length* 20 (20.5, 21, 22, 23.5, 23.75)(24.25, 24.25, 24.25, 25.5, 25.5)"

# Glossary

## Common Stitches & Techniques

### Slipped Stitches (Sl)
Always slip stitches purl-wise with yarn held to the wrong side of work, unless noted otherwise in the pattern.

### Make 1 Left-Leaning Stitch (M1L)
Inserting LH needle from front to back, PU the horizontal strand between the st just worked and the next st, and K TBL.

### Make 1 Right-Leaning Stitch (M1R)
Inserting LH needle from back to front, PU the horizontal strand between the st just worked and the next st, and K TFL.

### Slip, Slip, Knit (SSK)
(Sl1 K-wise) twice; insert LH needle into front of these 2 sts and knit them together.

### Centered Double Decrease (CDD)
Slip first and second sts together as if to work K2tog; K1; pass 2 slipped sts over the knit st.

### Stockinette Stitch (St st, flat over any number of sts)
Row 1 (RS): Knit all sts.
Row 2 (WS): Purl all sts.
Rep Rows 1–2 for pattern.
*St st in the round: Knit every rnd.*
Rev St st is the opposite—purl on RS, knit on WS.

### Garter Stitch (in the round over any number of sts)
Rnd 1: Purl all sts.
Rnd 2: Knit all sts.
Rep Rnds 1–2 for pattern.
*Garter Stitch flat: Knit every row.*
(One Garter *ridge* is comprised of two rows/rnds.)

### 1x1 Rib (flat or in the round, over an even number of sts)
Row/Rnd 1: (K1, P1) to end of row/rnd.
Rep Row/Rnd 1 for pattern.

### 2x2 Rib (flat over a multiple of 4 sts plus 2)
Row 1 (RS): K2, (P2, K2) to end of row.
Row 2 (WS): P2, (K2, P2) to end of row.
Rep Rows 1–2 for pattern.

### 2x2 Rib (in the round over a multiple of 4 sts)
Rnd 1: (K2, P2) to end of rnd.
Rep Rnd 1 for pattern.

### Knitting in the Round
The Magic Loop technique uses one long circular needle to knit around a small circumference. The Two Circulars technique uses two long circular needles to knit around a small circumference. Photo and video tutorials for these, plus using DPNs and 16" circular needles, can be found at knitpicks.com/learning-center/knitting-in-round.

### Backwards Loop Cast On
A simple, all-purpose cast on that can be worked mid-row. Also called Loop or Single Cast On. A tutorial can be found at knitpicks.com/learning-center/backwards-loop-cast-on.

### Long Tail Cast On
Fast and neat once you get the hang of it. Also referred to as the Slingshot Cast On. A tutorial can be found at knitpicks.com/learning-center/learn-to-knit.

### Cable Cast On
A strong and nice looking basic cast on that can be worked mid-project. A tutorial can be found at tutorials.knitpicks.com/cabled-cast-on.

### Knitted Cast On
A basic cast on that can be worked mid-project. A tutorial can be found at knitpicks.com/learning-center/knitted-cast-on.

### 3-Needle Bind Off
Used to easily seam two rows of live stitches together. A tutorial can be found at knitpicks.com/learning-center/3-needle-bind-off.

---

## Abbreviations

| | | | | | | | |
|---|---|---|---|---|---|---|---|
| approx | approximately | KFB *(inc 1)* | knit into front and back of stitch | PSSO *(dec 1)* | pass slipped stitch over | SSP *(dec 1)* | slip, slip, purl these 2 stitches together through back loop |
| BO | bind off | K-wise | knit-wise | PU | pick up | | |
| BOR | beginning of round | LH | left hand | P-wise | purl-wise | SSSK *(dec 2)* | slip, slip, slip, knit these 3 stitches together (like SSK) |
| CN | cable needle | M | marker | rep | repeat | | |
| C (1, 2...) | color (1, 2...) | M1 *(inc 1)* | make 1 stitch (work same as M1L) | Rev St st | reverse stockinette stitch *(see above)* | St st | stockinette stitch *(see above)* |
| CC | contrast color | | | | | | |
| CDD *(dec 2)* | centered double decrease *(see above)* | M1L *(inc 1)* | make 1 left-leaning stitch *(see above)* | RH | right hand | st(s) | stitch(es) |
| | | | | rnd(s) | round(s) | TBL | through back loop |
| CO | cast on | M1R *(inc 1)* | make 1 right-leaning stitch *(see above)* | RS | right side | TFL | through front loop |
| cont | continue | | | Sk | skip | tog | together |
| dec(s) | decrease(es) | MC | main color | SK2P *(dec 2)* | slip 1, knit 2 together, pass slipped stitch over | W&T | wrap & turn *(see next page)* |
| DPN(s) | double pointed needle(s) | P | purl | | | | |
| | | P2tog *(dec 1)* | purl 2 stitches together | SKP *(dec 1)* | slip, knit, pass slipped stitch over | WE | work even |
| inc(s) | increase(s) | | | | | WS | wrong side |
| K | knit | P3tog *(dec 2)* | purl 3 stitches together | Sl | slip *(see above)* | WYIB | with yarn in back |
| K2tog *(dec 1)* | knit 2 stitches together | | | SM | slip marker | WYIF | with yarn in front |
| | | PM | place marker | SSK *(dec 1)* | slip, slip, knit these 2 stitches together *(see above)* | YO *(inc 1)* | bring yarn over needle from front up over to back |
| K3tog *(dec 2)* | knit 3 stitches together | PFB *(inc 1)* | purl into front and back of stitch | | | | |

## Cables

Tutorials for different kinds of cables, including 1 over 1 and 2 over 2, with and without cable needles, can be found at knitpicks.com/learning-center/guides/cables.

## Felted Join (to splice yarn)

One method for joining a new length of yarn to the end of one that is already being used. A tutorial can be found at tutorials.knitpicks.com/felted-join.

## Mattress Stitch

A neat, invisible seaming method that uses the bars between the first and second stitches on the edges. A tutorial can be found at tutorials.knitpicks.com/mattress-stitch.

## Provisional Cast On (crochet method)

Used to cast on stitches that are also a row of live stitches, so they can be put onto a needle and used later.

*Directions:* Using a crochet hook, make a slip knot, then hold knitting needle in left hand, hook in right. With yarn in back of needle, work a chain st by pulling yarn over needle and through chain st. Move yarn back to behind needle, and rep for the number of sts required. Chain a few more sts off the needle, then break yarn and pull end through last chain. (CO sts may be incorrectly mounted; if so, work into backs of these sts.) To unravel later (when sts need to be picked up), pull chain end out; chain should unravel, leaving live sts. A video tutorial can be found at tutorials.knitpicks.com /crocheted-provisional-cast-on.

## Provisional Cast On (crochet chain method)

Same result as the crochet method above, but worked differently, so you may prefer one or the other.

*Directions:* With a crochet hook, use scrap yarn to make a slip knot and chain the number of sts to be cast on, plus a few extra sts. Insert tip of knitting needle into first bump of crochet chain. Wrap project yarn around needle as if to knit, and pull yarn through crochet chain, forming first st. Rep this process until you have cast on the correct number of sts. To unravel later (when sts need to be picked up), pull chain out, leaving live sts. A photo tutorial can be found at tutorials.knitpicks.com/crocheted-provisional-cast-on.

## Judy's Magic Cast On

This method creates stitches coming out in opposite directions from a seamless center line, perfect for starting toe-up socks.

*Directions:* Make a slip knot and place loop around one of the two needles; anchor loop counts as first st. Hold needles tog, with needle that yarn is attached to on top. In other hand, hold yarn so tail goes over index finger and yarn attached to ball goes over thumb. Bring tip of bottom needle over strand of yarn on finger (top strand), around and under yarn and back up, making a loop around needle. Pull loop snug. Bring top needle (with slip knot) over yarn tail on thumb (bottom strand), around and under yarn and back up, making a loop around needle. Pull loop snug. Cont casting on sts until desired number is reached; top yarn strand always wraps around bottom needle, and bottom yarn strand always wraps around top needle. A tutorial can be found at tutorials.knitpicks.com/judys-magic-cast-on.

## Stretchy Bind Off

*Directions:* K2, *insert LH needle into front of 2 sts on RH needle and knit them tog—1 st remains on RH needle. K1; rep from * until all sts have been bound off. A tutorial can be found at tutorials.knitpicks.com/go-your-own-way-socks-toe-up-part-7-binding-off.

## Jeny's Surprisingly Stretchy Bind Off (for 1x1 Rib)

*Directions:* Reverse YO, K1, pass YO over; *YO, P1, pass YO and previous st over P1; reverse YO, K1, pass YO and previous st over K1; rep from * until 1 st is left, then break working yarn and pull it through final st to complete BO.

## Kitchener Stitch (also called Grafting)

Seamlessly join two sets of live stitches together.

*Directions:* With an equal number of sts on two needles, break yarn leaving a tail approx four times as long as the row of sts, and thread through a blunt yarn needle. Hold needles parallel with WSs facing in and both needles pointing to the right. Perform Step 2 on the first front st, then Step 4 on the first back st, then continue from Step 1, always pulling yarn tightly so the grafted row tension matches the knitted fabric:

**Step 1:** Pull yarn needle K-wise through front st and drop st from knitting needle.

**Step 2:** Pull yarn needle P-wise through next front st, leaving st on knitting needle.

**Step 3:** Pull yarn needle P-wise through first back st and drop st from knitting needle.

**Step 4:** Pull yarn needle K-wise through next back st, leaving st on knitting needle.

Rep Steps 1–4 until all sts have been grafted together, finishing by working Step 1 through the last remaining front st, then Step 3 through the last remaining back st. Photo tutorials can be found at knitpicks.com/learning-center/learn-to-knit/kitchener.

## Short Rows

There are several options for how to handle short rows, so you may see different suggestions/intructions in a pattern.

### Wrap and Turn (W&T) (one option for Short Rows)

Work until the st to be wrapped. If knitting: Bring yarn to front, Sl next st P-wise, return yarn to back; turn work, and Sl wrapped st onto RH needle. Cont across row. If purling: Bring yarn to back of work, Sl next st P-wise, return yarn to front; turn work and Sl wrapped st onto RH needle. Cont across row.

**Picking up Wraps:** Work to wrapped st. If knitting: Insert RH needle under wrap, then through wrapped st K-wise; K st and wrap tog. If purling: Sl wrapped st P-wise onto RH needle, use LH needle to lift wrap and place it onto RH needle; Sl wrap and st back onto LH needle, and P tog.

A tutorial for W&T can be found at tutorials.knitpicks.com /short-rows-wrap-and-turn-or-wt.

### German Short Rows (another option for Short Rows)

Work to turning point; turn. WYIF, Sl first st P-wise. Bring yarn over back of right needle, pulling firmly to create a "double stitch" on RH needle. If next st is a K st, leave yarn at back; if next st is a P st, bring yarn to front between needles. When it's time to work into double st, knit both strands tog. A video tutorial for German Short Rows can be found at knitpicks.com/video/german-short-rows.

# THIS COLLECTION FEATURES

**Swish™**
Worsted Weight
100% Fine Superwash Merino Wool

**Twill™**
Worsted Weight
100% Superwash Merino Wool

**Woodland Tweed™**
Aran/Heavy Worsted Weight
80% Merino Wool, 15% Baby Alpaca, 5% Viscose

**Wool of the Andes™ Worsted & Tweed**
Worsted Weight
(Worsted) 100% Peruvian Highland Wool /
(Tweed) 80% Peruvian Highland Wool, 20% Donegal Tweed

View these beautiful
yarns and more at
www.KnitPicks.com

Knit Picks yarn is both luxe and affordable—a seeming contradic-
tion trounced! But it's not just about the pretty colors; we also care
deeply about fiber quality and fair labor practices, leaving you with
a gorgeously reliable product you'll turn to time and time again.

Knit Picks®

This collection of ten gender-neutral garments is everything a cable-loving knitter could hope for. Providing an extensive size range, most of these garments would be a great fit for any body, making this book perfect for extravagant gift-knitting options. With their variety of construction styles, shapes, and cable types, these patterns will hold the interest of advanced knitters and act as excellent level-up skill-builders for knitters newer to cables. Chalet is sure to keep your fingers busy and your body warm!

$29.99
ISBN 978-1-62767-278-8

52999>

9 781627 672788

33862